Color Guard of the 1st Delaware, taken at J.E. Torbert's Studio in Wilmington, probably in January of 1864. (Courtesy of the Historical Society of Delaware)

HISTORY
OF THE
FIRST REGIMENT,
DELAWARE VOLUNTEERS,

*FROM THE COMMENCEMENT OF THE
"THREE MONTHS' SERVICE" TO THE
FINAL MUSTER-OUT AT THE CLOSE
OF THE REBELLION.*

BY

WILLIAM P. SEVILLE,
CAPTAIN COMPANY "E," FIRST REGIMENT DELAWARE VOLUNTEERS

Longstreet House
Hightstown, N.J.
Reprint No. 213
1998

Originally printed, Wilmington, 1884
Reprinted by Longstreet House, 1986
Expanded reprint by Longstreet House, 1998

Please direct all correspondence and book orders to:
Longstreet House
P.O. Box 730
Hightstown, NJ 08520-0730

ISBN Number 0-944413-52-8

Printed in the United States of America

Contents

Illustrations

Editor's Preface

Longstreet House is pleased to present this expanded edition of its first reprint, our 1986 edition of William P. Seville's History of the First Regiment Delaware Volunteers. This fine little volume was long unavailable, and most surviving original copies are too fragile to use in their soft cover format. This was reprinted by us in hardback form in 1986. The present 1998 edition contains a new photographic supplement with maps, and an enlarged textual format. Hopefully it will promote further interest in the First Delaware Infantry and will help promote additional study of this excellent but long neglected regiment.

Thanks are owed to the Historical Society of Delaware, the U.S. Army Military History Institute, Jeff Kowalis and William A. McKay for permission to use photographs from their collections.

Dr. David G. Martin
Hightstown, New Jersey
January 1998

Edwin H. Bryan. 1st Lieutenant, Company A. Regimental Quartermaster, March 1, 1863. Brevet Captain, April 9, 1865. (William A. McKay Collection)

Martin W.B. Ellegood. Captain, Company E. Mortally wounded at Gettysburg, July 2, 1863, and died two days later. (Jeff Kowalis collection)

Thomas V. England. 1st Lieutenant, Regimental
Quartermaster. Captain and Commissary of Substance,
March 1, 1863. (U.S. Army Military History Institute)

x

Albert Gawthorp. 1st Lieutenant, Company G. Resigned
September 16, 1862, for disability. (U.S. Army Military
History Institute)

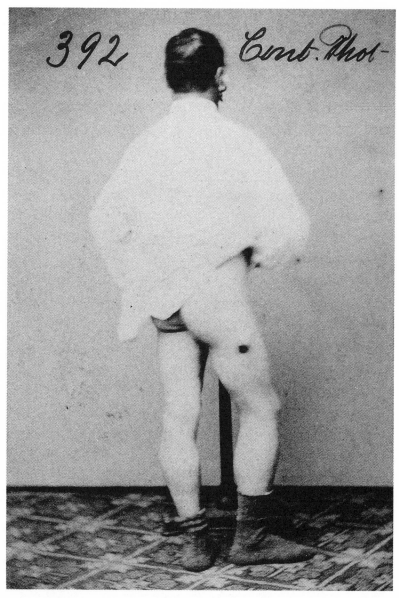

John Hamilton, of Company I, was 19 years old when he was accidentally wounded in the upper right thigh by a fellow soldier while on picket duty the night of November 10, 1861. He recovered, but the wound caused a one inch shortening of the leg. This photo was taken in April 1865 as part of an army medical study. (William A. McKay Collection)

John W. Johnson. Corporal, Company D, 1st Delaware
Veteran Volunteers, 1864. (William A. McKay Collection)

Samuel A. MacAllister. Sergeant, Company F. Sergeant
Major, December 18,1862. 2nd Lieutenant, Company B. 1st
Lieutenant, Company F, January 20, 1863. Also served as
aide-de-camp to General Thomas A. Smyth. (William A.
McKay Collection)

William Marsh. Sergeant, Company C. 1st Lieutenant, Company F, June 9, 1865. (U.S. Army Military History Institute)

David W. Maull. Surgeon. Also served as Surgeon in Chief
for 3rd Brigade, 2nd Division, II Corps. Resigned April
20,1865. (U.S. Army Military History Institute)

Francis McCloskey. 1st Lieutenant, Company C. Resigned
November 1, 1861. (U.S. Army Military History Institute)

George T. Price. Sergeant, Company G. 2nd Lieutenant, Company A, March 11, 1863. 1st Lieutenant, July 3,1863. Captain, Company C, November 6,1863. Discharged, May 15,1865 (U.S. Army Military History Institute)

William P. Seville, author of this history, served as adjutant of the three months' regiment and also of the three years' regiment. He was promoted to Captain of Company E on September 21, 1863, where he served until the termination of his enlistment on October 11, 1864. (U.S. Army Military History Institute)

Thomas A. Smyth. Major, October 17, 1861. Lieutenant
Colonel, December 30, 1862, Colonel, February 7, 1863.
Held brigade command in the II Corps after Chancellorsville
and division command in 1864-1865. Brigadier General,
U.S.V., October 1, 1864. Mortally wounded near Farmville,
Va., April 7, 1865, and died April 9. Brevet Major General
posthumously. (William A. McKay Collection)

John L. Sparks. 2nd Lieutenant, Company G. I 1st Lieutenant, September 16, 1862. Captain, Company K, January 20, 1863. Also served as aide-de-camp to General Thomas A. Smyth. (U.S. Army Military History Institute)

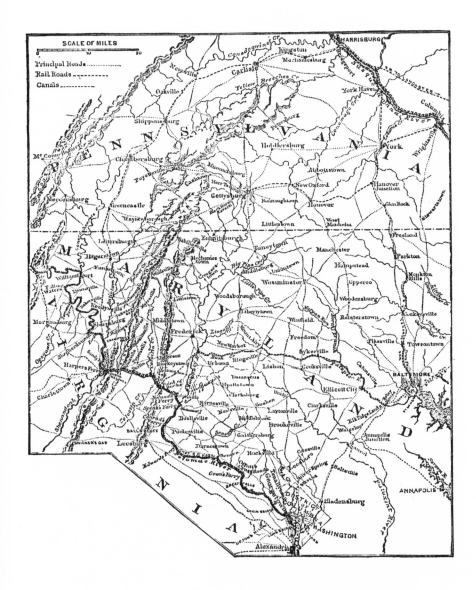

Map of the Virginia Campaigns (*Battles and Leaders of the Civil War*)

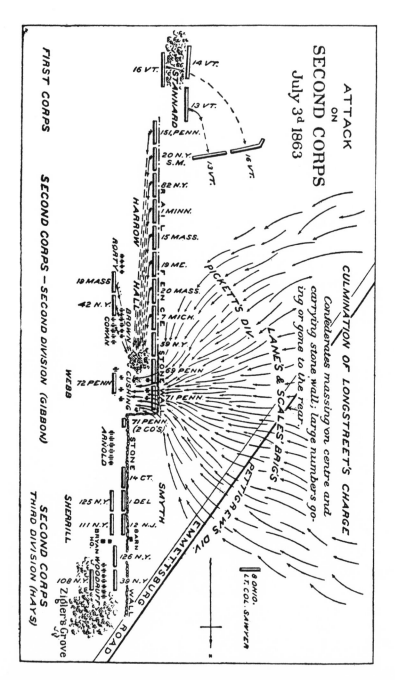

Position of the 1st Delaware on July 3, 1863 at Gettysburg
(Walker, History of the Second Army Corps)

POSITION
HELD BY
THE 1st REG.
DEL. VOL.
INFANTRY
2nd BRIG. 3rd DIV.
2nd ARMY CORPS
JULY 2nd
AND 3rd
1863.

ERECTED BY THE STATE OF
DELAWARE TO COMMEMORATE
THE GALLANTRY OF
HER SONS.
A.D. 1885.

Monument of the 1st Delaware on Cemetery Ridge at Gettysburg (Wert, *A Complete Handbook of the Monuments... on the Gettysburg Battlefield*)

HISTORY

OF THE

FIRST REGIMENT,

DELAWARE VOLUNTEERS,

FROM THE COMMENCEMENT OF THE "THREE MONTHS' SERVICE"
TO THE FINAL MUSTER-OUT AT THE CLOSE
OF THE REBELLION.

BY

WILLIAM P. SEVILLE,

CAPTAIN COMPANY "E," FIRST REGIMENT DELAWARE VOLUNTEERS.

ON the 22d of April, 1873, the colors of the Second, Third, Fourth, and Fifth Delaware Regiments, which served in the War of the Rebellion, were turned over to the Historical Society of Delaware for safe custody. The colors were presented by Major-General Hancock, on behalf of the regiments, and were received by William C. Spruance, Esq., as the representative of the Society, in the presence of a large assembly in the Opera-House in the city of Wilmington.

On the 29th of January, 1884, the colors carried by the First Delaware Regiment during the last three eventful years of the war, were deposited in the Rooms of the Society, subject to the orders of the Regimental Association. The ceremony of delivery was informal, and, in consequence of inclement weather and defective notice, very few persons were present on the occasion. At a subsequent meeting of the Society, on motion of Dr. L. P. Bush, a resolution was adopted to the effect that the Council of the First Delaware Regiment Association be requested to prepare a brief history of the regiment for the use of the Society. Captain W. P. Seville was selected by his comrades for the performance of this duty, and on May 19, 1884, that gentleman read the material portions of the following paper before the survivors of the regiment, the members of the Society and invited guests.

Captain Seville was well qualified for the task assigned to him from the fact that he took a prominent part in organizing the First Delaware Regiment for three months' service, and also in its reorganization for three years. He was adjutant of both regiments, was afterwards appointed captain of Company E, and from the spring of 1862 served on the staffs of General T. A. Smyth and Colonel Allbright until his discharge, October 30, 1864.

A complete Muster-Roll of the First Regiment, made under the supervision of General J. Parke Postles, was also deposited with the colors.

HISTORY

OF

THE FIRST REGIMENT,

DELAWARE VOLUNTEERS.

THE THREE MONTHS' CAMPAIGN.

In the spring of 1861, when the forebodings of the people that the political differences of the nation would culminate in civil strife had settled into a hopeless conviction, the citizens of Delaware were enjoying a reasonable share of prosperity, and, if we except the excitement of party issues, were comparatively tranquil.

The question of slavery, the rock on which our ship of state had struck, was, however, one of too great magnitude, and was too deeply rooted in its principles, not to affect very seriously the feelings and interests of the people of Delaware. Its citizens were closely united in habits, sympathies, and interests with that portion of our people dwelling in the gulf and cotton-raising States. Delaware itself was, in fact, a slave State at this time, and nearly all of the customs appertaining to this " peculiar institution" still exercised potent sway, although the signs of the times during the twenty

years then closing clearly indicated that the slave-holding
system had fallen into a rapid decline, and, at no very distant day, would be completely eradicated through the opera-
tion of natural causes alone.

The first census taken in Delaware, in 1790, showed the
number of slaves in the State to be 8887. This number
gradually diminished, and the census of 1860 disclosed the
fact that the entire State then owned but 1798 slaves. Of
these, 1341 were held in Sussex County, 254 in New Castle
County, and 203 in Kent County, showing that the favorite
institution of the South had a much firmer hold in Sussex
than it had in either of the other counties. And thus it
was that Sussex County exercised a powerful and almost
controlling influence in the politics of the State; so that
when the momentous questions involved in the fierce sec-
tional quarrel obtruded themselves on the attention of the
people in 1860, and reason abdicated its throne in despair of
reaching either a satisfactory settlement or an honorable
compromise,—when the tumultuous passions which reigned
supreme abandoned the forum and sought the sanguinary
field, the State of Delaware, though the best interests of its
citizens were identified with the free principles which obtained throughout the North, was influenced to some extent
by the positive utterances and defiant conduct of a few men
whose hopes of gain and preferment were bound up in the
fate of the South, and fears were entertained that disloyalty
would raise its head in the halls of the Legislature and an
act of secession be passed.

It was in these troublous times, when loyalty seemed
to pervade the hearts of the people, and all eyes were

strained to welcome the men who should step forth and disclose the requisite boldness and ability to resist the undercurrent that was drifting the State towards certain destruction, that the much-needed patriots appeared. Several among the more prominent citizens in all parts of the State, but more particularly in New Castle County, ventured to discuss the vital question in a public manner, setting clearly before the people at public assemblages, and through the mediumship of the press, the undeniable advantages that would accrue to the State by continuing true in its allegiance to the established government, appealing to the patriotism of the people, and depicting in faithful colors the horrors and suffering that would overtake the citizens of Delaware if the State should attempt to leave the Union, and be made the battle-ground of the contending armies.

These manifestations of loyalty began to take form in the efforts made in April, 1861, to organize a regiment for the defence of the Union. For some weeks there had been a growing conviction that the great national trouble, then nearing a crisis, would scarcely be dispelled without some effusion of blood in the duty of suppressing insurrection; but the most extreme among the prophets of evil hardly ventured to predict such madness on the part of the secession leaders as would drive them to indulge in any act of opposition to the general government of a more serious nature than that of *threatening* disruption of the Union by force of arms. Such demonstrations were regarded as mere *brutum fulmen*, the intemperate vaporings of a disappointed political clique; but when State after State adopted ordinances of secession; when armed bodies were organized and drilled; when the note of hostile preparation rose on every hand in the rebellious States; and, finally, when a furious force set itself in battle array before Fort Sumter, and the dreadful overture to civil war was begun on the morning of Friday, April 12, 1861, by the opening of the rebel guns on that work and the revered national flag, all doubts were instantly dissipated.

The patriots of Delaware, with those of the other loyal States, accepted the wager of battle thus thrown down by the infatuated foe. Burning with indignation at the outrage committed upon the national government and a desire to avenge that disgrace, they rallied to their country's defence.

Throughout the Northern States the initiative in organizing troops was taken promptly and effectively by their respective State governments, which at once provided officers to organize the volunteers, and made the necessary arrangements for furnishing them with arms, provisions, and clothing. This timely action resulted in placing in the field a respectable force within a fortnight after the call of the President for volunteers, on the 15th of April, 1861, and by this means the patriotic earnestness of the people was quickly utilized, and the first quota of troops was concentrating at the national capital on the 18th, just three days from the date of the proclamation.

The loyal men of Delaware, however, had not the assistance of the State government in preparing to defend the country. With an intense desire to be among the first to plant their standard before the defiant foe, they were prevented from the accomplishment of this patriotic purpose

through want of the requisite aid in the work of organization.   To men actuated by the liveliest patriotism and the
most indomitable zeal, the lack of official aid could not
long prove an obstacle to success.   Measures having once
been taken to form a regiment for national defence, many
warm-hearted and loyal men and women came forward to
assist in the laudable work; and, while men engaged themselves in the labor of finding means of supplying subsistence
through the liberality of the patriotic citizens, the ladies
were equally earnest and successful in furnishing clothing
and other necessary stores for the support of the volunteers.

The laws of Delaware contained no provision for maintaining militia organizations, and when the Governor was
called on by the Secretary of War to furnish one regiment
as the quota of the State, the following proclamation was
issued by Governor Burton, April 23, 1861, viz.:

" Whereas, a requisition has been made upon the undersigned, as Executive
of the said State of Delaware, by the Secretary of War, for one regiment,
consisting of seven hundred and eighty men, to be immediately detached
from the militia of this State, to serve as infantry or riflemen for the period
of three months, unless sooner discharged; and, whereas, the laws of this
State do not confer upon the Executive any authority enabling him to comply
with said requisition, there being no organized militia, nor any law requiring
such organization; and, whereas, it is the duty of all good and law-abiding
citizens to preserve the peace and sustain the laws and government under
which we live and by which our citizens are protected :—Therefore, I, William
Burton, Governor of the said State of Delaware, recommend the formation
of volunteer companies for the protection of the lives and property of the
people of this State against violence of any sort to which they may be exposed.
For these purposes, such companies, when formed, will be under the control
of the State authorities, though not subject to be ordered by the Executive
into the United States service,—the law not vesting in him such authority.

They will, however, have the option of offering their services to the general government, for the defence of its capital and the support of the Constitution and laws of the country.

" WILLIAM BURTON."

In response to this call three companies were immediately enrolled, and, as a large number of men were ready to volunteer, who were prevented from organizing only through the lack of qualified and capable leaders, the more thoughtful and energetic of those who had been intrusted with the direction of affairs addressed themselves to the duty of seeking for men possessed of sufficient military knowledge to form these volunteers into companies and organize the regiment; their efforts were at length successful, and by the end of April four companies were formed in Wilmington and New Castle, and several others had begun the work of enrollment.

The Governor, having been informed that the required regiment could be speedily obtained, issued the subjoined order, viz. :

" DOVER, DELAWARE, May 1, 1861.

" The undersigned, the constitutional commander of the forces of the State of Delaware, directs that those volunteer companies of the State that desire to be mustered into the service of the United States, under the call of the President, will rendezvous to the city of Washington with the least possible delay, where they will be mustered into the service of the United States by Major Ruff, who has been detailed by the War Department for that purpose, and who has reported himself to me and received my instructions. The regiment will consist of ten companies, to serve for the period of three months.

" WILLIAM BURTON,
" Governor and Commander-in-Chief."

THE WORK OF ORGANIZATION.

During the political campaign of 1860 party spirit, as before remarked, ran very high. The most determined efforts were used by popular leaders to spur every man up to the performance of his duty. One of the prominent features of the campaign was the formation of clubs, familiarly known as "Wide Awakes," "Bell Men," and "Minute Men." These bodies, besides being distinguished by peculiar uniforms, were thoroughly exercised in tactics similar to those used in military service. From these bands sprang the enrollment of the first companies of volunteers in the city of Wilmington, and thus the First Regiment of Delaware Volunteers had its birth.

One of these Bell and Everett clubs was commanded by Robert S. La Motte, and another by Charles E. La Motte. When the call of the President was published, on the 19th of April, these gentlemen promptly responded, and at once commenced to raise companies from among the members of the before-mentioned clubs. Two companies were speedily filled to their maximum strength, and were designated as Companies A and B, the former commanded by Robert S. La Motte, and the latter by his brother Charles.

Through the exertions of the Messrs. La Motte, and other patriotic citizens of Wilmington, the "Institute Building," on Market Street, was secured as an armory and quarters for the troops. Here the duty of drilling and disciplining the men was at once entered upon, which, owing to the want of arms, was necessarily confined to the movements and evolutions of the squad and company.

About the same time the formation of these companies was begun the nucleus of another company was formed in Wilmington by Joseph M. Barr, which, having soon after reached its full strength, was assigned as Company C in the regimental line. Several other companies were in course of formation in the lower counties, the commanding officers of which were eagerly inquiring at Dover and Wilmington in what manner they were to proceed to Washington with their companies.

The State of Delaware was in the district commanded by General Robert Patterson, whose headquarters were in Philadelphia, Pa. This officer having been apprised of the formation of three or four companies at Wilmington, issued an order placing Captain R. S. La Motte in command of the battalion, and directing him to proceed with all possible diligence to organize the regiment. At this time, the work of consolidation was retarded by the want of some person having a knowledge of army organization to combine the several companies into a regimental body, and the friends of Captain Alfred J. Pleasonton, of Delaware (an officer in the United States Army, who was the choice of many officers for colonel), were endeavoring to obtain the consent of the War Department to his acceptance of the command of the regiment. Captain Pleasonton, who was extremely desirous of obtaining the command of the first regiment from Delaware, was in Philadelphia in the latter part of April seeking to further the object in view, and hasten to Wilmington to engage in the work of organization.

It was at this time that Captain Pleasonton made the acquaintance of Captain William P. Seville, who commanded a company in Philadelphia then waiting to be mustered in.   As Mr. Seville had received a military education in the army, and was fresh from West Point, where he had been attached to the Engineer Corps, Captain Pleasonton induced him to resign his command in Philadelphia and cast his fortunes in with the Delaware troops, and furnished him with a letter of introduction to acting Major R. S. La Motte, at the same time informing Mr. Seville that he hoped and expected to command the regiment.

Mr. Seville proceeded to Wilmington on the 2d of May, and was received with great cordiality by acting Major La Motte, who at once issued an order announcing his appointment as acting adjutant of the battalion.   For two weeks the drills and instruction of Companies A and B at the Institute were carried on with unflagging zeal, and the " Fair Grounds" in the suburbs of the city having been secured for a camp-ground, and named Camp Brandywine, on the 22d of May three companies, A, B, and C, were marched out and quartered in tents and some sheds that had been hurriedly erected for their accommodation.   On the same day, the officers assembled and held an election for field-officers.   It having been authoritatively announced that Captain Pleasonton could not secure the permission of the Secretary of War to take the command, the election resulted in the choice of Henry H. Lockwood, then a Professor of Mathematics, and Instructor of Infantry Tactics in the United States Naval Academy at Annapolis, Md., as Colonel; John W. Andrews, Lieutenant-Colonel, and Henry A. Du Pont, Major.

On the 23d of May all the other companies came to the

camp but Company D, which did not report until the next day. The task of drilling, pitching tents, military arrangement of camp, and instruction in guard duty was immediately begun, and the men, profoundly impressed with the novelty of their new life and the difficulties of studying an entirely new profession, took an ardent interest in their duties and made rapid progress in the school of the soldier.

The night of the 23d of May was made memorable by one of those panics which are so liable to seize bodies of newly-instructed troops. A great commotion was created by some wags outside of the inclosure throwing stones into the camp. By the time the officers reached the scene of confusion several hundred men were rushing toward the spot from which the missiles came, guns in hand, fully determined to wreak dire vengeance on the disturbers of their peace and dignity. A few words sufficed to induce them to return to their quarters and intrust the duty of discovering and punishing the offenders to their officers.

Sunday, May 26th, the regiment attempted its first full dress-parade before an immense concourse of the citizens of Wilmington, and the nervousness of many of the officers to acquit themselves with credit in front of such a dangerous battery of fair eyes as then confronted them is, doubtless, an experience that will long linger in their memory. Lieutenant-Colonel Andrews arrived in camp on the 27th and assumed the command.

The regiment being now completed, excepting the staff, the following list comprises its officers as they were at that date :

Colonel, Henry H. Lockwood.

Lieutenant-Colonel, John W. Andrews.

Major, Henry A. Du Pont.

Company A.—Captain, Robert S. La' Motte; First Lieutenant, Evan S. Watson; Second Lieutenant, Franklin Houseman.

Company B.—Captain, Charles E. La Motte; First Lieutenant, James Plunkett; Second Lieutenant, Alfred Vandever.

Company C.—Captain, Joseph M. Barr; First Lieutenant, W. C. McKaig; Second Lieutenant, R. J. Holt.

Company D.—Captain, James Green; First Lieutenant, Enoch J. Smithers; Second Lieutenant, Samuel Simpson.

Company E.—Captain, Robert Milligan; First Lieutenant, Benjamin Nields; Second Lieutenant, Leonard E. Wales.

Company F.—Captain, Thomas Crossley; First Lieutenant, Richard Duncan; Second Lieutenant, William Plunkett.

Company G.—Captain, C. Rodney Layton; First Lieutenant, David W. Maull; Second Lieutenant, William Y. Swiggett.

Company H.—Captain, Samuel H. Jenkins; First Lieutenant, John H. Knight; Second Lieutenant, Daniel Woodall.

Company I.—Captain, James Leonard; First Lieutenant, John Daugherty; Second Lieutenant, Daniel Langdon.

Company K.—Captain, George F. Smith; First Lieutenant, Charles Bird; Second Lieutenant, W. H. Cleaden.

On May 28th we were thrown into a high fever of excitement by the receipt of marching orders for a portion of the command. The instructions were to station two companies at Aberdeen and two at Bush River, on the Philadelphia, Wilmington and Baltimore Railroad, to relieve companies of the Eleventh Pennsylvania Volunteers, Colonel Jarratt. For this service Companies A, B, E, and D were selected, and marched through the city to the depot on the same afternoon, conducted by acting Adjutant Seville. Companies A and B were stationed at Aberdeen, and D and E at Bush River. The latter detachment did not reach their destination until quite late; the Pennsylvania men had retired for the night in the only building that would afford shelter, and our newly-fledged soldiers were compelled to roll themselves in their blankets and take to the ground, much to their surprise and disgust.

The following day the Pennsylvania troops departed and vacated the quarters, and the day was spent in issuing rations and instructing the men and officers in guard duty. Great pains had been taken to have them fully understand the necessity of repeating the call for the sergeant of the guard by another sentinel, adding the number of the post. In the dead of the night a most deafening uproar arose, bringing every man out of bed in an instant. The sentries were firing at will and yelling like demons, while the men were tumbling out of the barracks in the direst confusion, each calling for some article of clothing or equipment that could not be found in the dark. When they rushed out of the building in wild excitement and found their officers standing there perfectly calm and collected, quietly directing them to fall into the ranks and finish dressing, they too sobered down, but showed in every action that they would give their knapsacks to know what, in the name of " old Nick," was going on. By the time the ranks were formed the racket among the sentries had been quieted down, and their officers, Captains Milligan and Green, availed themselves of the opportunity to deliver a lecture on discipline and self-possession, assuring them that, thereafter, they should bear in mind that no matter how vigorously the sentries called, it was the sergeant of the guard who was wanted, and not them. It was then explained to them that one of the sentries on the bridge had ordered a negro in a boat to stop, which he neglected to do, and so excited the sentinel that he fired at him and fairly howled for the officer of the guard, all the others repeating the alarm as well as they could hear it.

In the mean time Colonel Lockwood had reached the camp at Wilmington, and on the 31st of May appointed the staff, commissioned and non-commissioned. These were as follows, viz.:

> Adjutant, William P. Seville.
> Quartermaster, W. Hill Alderdice.
> Surgeon, Robert P. Johnson.
> Assistant Surgeon, James Knight.
> Chaplain, Rev. George M. Condron.
> Sergeant-Major, John G. Saville.

DEPARTURE FOR THE FRONT.

June 7th and 8th arms and accoutrements were issued to the companies last to arrive, and the remaining companies were inspected. The regiment left camp on the 9th, and marched through Wilmington to the depot, where it took the cars at 3 P.M. for its post of occupation along the rail-road through Maryland. Company G, Captain Layton, was dropped at Elkton; Company K, Captain Smith, was left at North East; and Companies C and H, Captains Barr and Jenkins, were dropped at Perryville. The other com-panies, F and I, continued to Havre de Grace, and went into camp and barracks.

From day to day the companies stationed nearest to Havre de Grace (which became headquarters) were brought in for battalion drill. One day an enterprising quartette, consisting of Captain R. S. La Motte, Chaplain Condron, Sergeant-Major Saville, and the adjutant, went on a forced march three miles down the railroad, surrounded the house of a farmer and captured a flag, which proved to be a home-made banner lacking the proper number of stars and stripes. The farmer explained that it was intended for the United States flag, and it was, if his daughter knew how to make one. The assailing party concluded that it looked enough like a secession flag to do duty for one, and so brought it along as a trophy.

June 11th it was announced to the regiment that Major Du Pont, who was an officer in the regular army, would not be allowed to accept the commission to which he was elected, whereupon an election was held, and Captain R. S. La Motte was promoted to fill the vacancy. Lieutenant E. S. Watson became captain of Company A, and Sergeant Ezekiel C. Alexander was elected first lieutenant.

A band was organized on the 18th of June, for which Lieutenant-Colonel Andrews purchased the instruments, and this musical attachment did more to subdue the disloyal stubbornness of the dwellers in Havre de Grace than all the bayonets of the command. About this time a small steamboat was placed at the order of Colonel Lockwood, to facilitate the sending of expeditions to points along the shores of the Susquehanna River and Chesapeake Bay; and the first use made of it was to set out on a reconnoissance up the river to Port Deposit, the force consisting of a dozen officers and the band. As no rebel works were encountered during the trip, a serenade was given to Mr. Tomes, residing there, who was evidently taken by surprise, for, on responding to his invitation to enter, a large table bountifully spread with choice refreshments, both edible and potable, was presented to view.

The next expedition steamed down the bay, and did not stop short of Annapolis, where a sumptuous supper was enjoyed at the house of Mr. Sprogle; after which a visit was paid to the executive mansion, and having, as usual, been introduced by the band, the expeditionary force was cordially invited in, heard from Governor Hicks his very interesting account of the exciting times when the secessionists of the State tried to run away with it, and drank success and prosperity to him, and plenty of it.

All the companies at Havre de Grace left on June 24th and went to Harewood, between Gunpowder River and Stemmer's Run; Companies B and K were stationed at Back River, and the others, F, H, C, and I, pitched their camp in a dense wood. Headquarters continued at Havre de Grace, and the band was carried up and down the road, spending a day with each of the detachments, to help mitigate the rigors of camp-life. On one visit it made to

Bush River, a sloop was obtained by the officers, and a military expedition was planned to scout up the river, accompanied by the band; as no enemy was met with prepared to do battle, they went ashore at a mansion, which proved to be the house of a Mr. Wainright, and fired away (uselessly, as it turned out) several of their very best tunes; for neither Mr. Wainright nor any of his family appeared to have any soul for music,—that is, the music of the Union.

The first loss to the regiment occurred on the 11th of July: Major La Motte received an appointment as captain in the regular army, and left us for his new field of duty. We felt his loss deeply, for his genial and soldierly qualities had endeared him to all his comrades, both officers and privates. An election resulted in the promotion of Captain C. Rodney Layton to fill the vacancy.

For a week or two at this time the monotony of camp duty and drill was relieved by a succession of exciting events. On the 19th the Sixth Maine Regiment passed through Havre de Grace on its way to the front. Some of them conceived that a German baker, named Harpst, wanted to poison them with the bread he sold them, and we had much difficulty to save the poor frightened Teuton from instant destruction. Then one of the members of the Maine regiment was accidentally shot, and was left at the hotel, where he died next day, and was buried with all the honors by our regiment. On the 22d of July we heard the news of the disaster at Bull Run, which sadly depressed our spirits, and greatly elated the majority of the dwellers in Havre de Grace. The animated discussions over this

sad reverse to our arms invariably resulted in a vehement
expression of opinion that we had no business to be left
idling our time away guarding a railroad track when we
were so badly needed in the field.   Colonel Lockwood did
make an eloquent and urgent appeal to the War Department, beseeching that the First Delaware might be ordered
into action before the expiration of our time, and was
informed in reply that the duty the regiment was performing was quite as valuable to the country, and fully as
honorable to the men engaged in it, as any that could be
rendered elsewhere.   As a climax to these sensations, one
of another character was furnished by Company I on the
23d of July.   That company having had a short interview
with the paymaster, found nothing of any value to them
in the vicinity to purchase excepting an article which was
commonly known among them as " eye-water;" and, to
judge from the quantity of this medicine they laid in, one
would have thought their barracks was a blind asylum, for,
to tell the truth, many of them were " blind" before the day
closed.   As is usual with men of the nationality which
furnished most of the membership of Company I, a jolly
time would lose half of its enjoyment without a fight, and
they had one,—a regular family row.   This was summarily suppressed by the guard, and the cellar of the building,
which was used by the field and staff as a mess-hall, was
turned into a guard-house, and well filled with these roys-
tering boys.   A day or two after, when their money was all
gone, the colonel sent Company I to Back River, and
brought Companies B and K to headquarters.

The time of service of Companies A, B, C, D, and E

expired on August 2d, and the men were seized with an intense desire to go home. They requested the colonel to relieve them and permit them to return to Delaware at once; but he endeavored to persuade them that it would have a far better appearance if they would tarry two weeks longer and march home with the entire regimental organization; they persisting, however, the colonel surrendered the point, and, on the following day, these five companies left the tented field and hastened home; not to relapse into inglorious ease, and participate in the great national struggle for human liberty and free government, only by reading the accounts of battles in the newspapers,—not they: but to enter again into the work of recruiting companies for another bout with the enemy, where they could give and take hard blows, instead of mounting guard over a lot of switches and round-houses.

The time of Company F expired on the 8th of August, and they also turned their faces homeward. The regiment was honored at this time by the appointment of Colonel Lockwood to be brigadier-general of volunteers. The officers, as well as the rank and file, felt a just pride in furnishing from the regiment a general officer after but three months' service; and, being full of enthusiasm and military ardor, they doubtless thought that if generals were to spring from the Delaware troops in future every three months, there was a wide field for ambition, and an additional incentive to re-entering the service for three years.

Colonel Lockwood, however, had won his promotion by able and faithful service. A highly-educated and refined gentleman, of dignified mien and commanding presence, the few months during which he commanded the regiment were sufficient to reveal his efficiency as a military leader, and to demonstrate the wisdom of selecting him for the exercise of more important commands. As the first citizen of Delaware to reach the distinction of brigadier-general, the State naturally felt proud of him. His subsequent service in the field showed him to be a brave officer, and his administrative ability gained him the honor of commanding the Middle Military Department.

Reports having been received at headquarters from one of those prolific sources of startling intelligence which came to be so well known during that period of the war ("a reliable gentleman") that a large collection of arms and ammunition was concealed in the vicinity of the Sassafras River near the bay, it was determined to send a force to scour that neighborhood, and, if the military stores could be found, to capture them. Accordingly, seventy men, principally volunteers, with the proper quota of officers, embarked on the steamboat in the middle of the night of the 11th of August (this time without the band), steamed quietly down the bay, and approached their point of destination in the gray dawn. The officers and men were kept concealed, and none were visible but the pilot and two or three men attired in the peaceful uniform of roustabouts. The force landed and marched three or four miles into the enemy's country, but no battery, arms, ammunition, nor enemy of any description were discovered, and the expedition returned to camp to relate what would have been done had any opposition been encountered.

At last the day arrived which witnessed the close of our

bloodless though active campaign. On August 13th the Fourth New York (Scott Life Guard) came to relieve us, and the men at once began preparations for marching on Wilmington and once more rush to arms,—the arms of loved ones at home.

The following day, August 14, 1861, saw the battalion paraded for the last roll-call, with clean uniforms, brightened arms, polished ornaments, and gleeful faces. The distance by railroad from the place of regimental rendezvous was but a few miles, consequently the command soon reached the city of Wilmington, and found their late comrades and a vast concourse of admiring friends assembled to give them a welcome and to listen " with bated breath" to their tales " of moving accidents by flood and field."

Thus ended the first term of service of the First Delaware Regiment; and if we brought not back with us decimated ranks and honorable scars, we were, at least, the proud recipients of warm commendations from officers of the government, who spoke in praise of the faithfulness with which the duty imposed upon the regiment had been performed; and one official of which, then high in command, had said, when the regiment was forming, " I would rather have one regiment from Delaware at this time than two from any other State."

REORGANIZATION.

As before intimated, recruiting-stations for the formation of companies for three years, unless sooner discharged, sprang up on every hand, opened by some of the commissioned officers of the three months' organization, and by several non-commissioned officers who aspired to the dignity of epaulets.

Lieutenant-Colonel Andrews, whose patriotism and whose martial proclivities led him to take a predominating interest in the labor of getting another regiment into the field from Delaware, was untiring in his efforts, and ever ready, with his knowledge of military affairs, to assist in completing the companies. Towards him, therefore, the eyes of the prospective line-officers naturally turned for a commanding officer. Colonel Andrews gratefully acknowledged the preference so generally expressed, accepted the responsibility, and entered zealously into the work before him. It was the unanimous wish of those who had served three months that the new organization should bear the old title, " First Delaware." This desire was inspired by the fact that more companies were in the field than could be embraced in one regiment; and it soon became evident that there would be two or more regiments ready for muster nearly about the same time, all of the competing companies having, among their officers or in their ranks, many members of the organization so recently disbanded.

At this juncture of affairs, Colonel Andrews applied to the War Department for authority to reorganize the First Regiment for the long term, which was promptly granted.

A regimental camping-ground was then secured at Hare's Corner, which was forthwith named Camp Andrews. To this pleasant grove each company proceeded as it reached the maximum, tents were pitched, and squad-drills commenced. On the last day of September all the companies had reported in camp, and an election was held for field-officers, all of whom were chosen excepting the lieutenant-colonel, which position, it was agreed, should be left vacant for a few days. After the field-officers had been selected the colonel appointed his staff and the non-commissioned staff. The officers of the regiment were then as follows, viz. :

Colonel, John W. Andrews.

Lieutenant-Colonel, ——— ———.

Major, Thomas A. Smyth.

Adjutant, William P. Seville.

Quartermaster, Thomas Y. England.

Surgeon, David W. Maull.

Assistant Surgeon, Samuel D. Marshall.

Chaplain, Thomas G. Murphey.

Sergeant-Major, James Lewis.

Quartermaster-Sergeant, Frank Wilson.

Commissary-Sergeant, Charles S. Schaeffer.

Hospital Steward, Archibald D. O'Mera.

Drum-Major, Patrick Dooley.

Principal Musician, John B. Ritchie.

Company A.—Captain, Evan S. Watson; First Lieutenant, James Parke Postles; Second Lieutenant, Franklin Houseman.

Company B.—Captain, James Leonard; First Lieutenant, James A. Oates; Second Lieutenant, James Rickards.

Company C.—Captain, Neal Ward; First Lieutenant, Frank McCloskey; Second Lieutenant, Hugh Sweeney.

Company D.—Captain, Enoch J. Smithers; First Lieutenant, David S. Yardley; Second Lieutenant, William F. Smith.

Company E.—Captain, Edward P. Harris; First Lieutenant, William Y. Swiggett; Second Lieutenant, Albert S. Phillips.

Company F.—Captain, Daniel Woodall; First Lieutenant, Benjamin E. Adams; Second Lieutenant, John W. Williams.

Company G.—Captain, Allen Shortledge; First Lieutenant, Alfred Gawthrop; Second Lieutenant, John L. Sparks.

Company H.—Captain, John B. Tanner; First Lieutenant, John R. Vanloan; Second Lieutenant, Ezekiel C. Alexander.

Company I.—Captain, Charles Lespés; First Lieutenant, Thomas B. Hizar; Second Lieutenant, Isaac Van Trump.

Company K.—Captain, Thomas Crossley; First Lieutenant, William C. Inhoff; Second Lieutenant, Henry H. Burton.

On the evening of October 8th the regiment had its first parade in undress uniforms, arms and equipments not having yet arrived, and next day orders were received to report to General John E. Wool, at Fort Monroe, on the earliest day practicable. Arms and accoutrements were received sufficient to equip eight companies on the 12th of October, and drilling at the manual of arms was begun. Inspection on company parade-grounds was held on the 13th, and a color-guard was selected. October 15th an election for lieutenant-colonel was held, and Mr. Oliver P. Hopkinson, of Philadelphia, Pa., was elected. Arms were furnished for the remaining companies, and the entire time was occupied in drill and camp duties until the 20th, on which day it had been determined by the colonel that the command should leave for the front. The 19th was a day of great activity and excitement in and around Camp Andrews, for not only was the regiment packing up for the move, but a host of self-constituted sutlers, who had spread their canvas and located their sheds outside of the camp limits, were also making preparations to remove their stocks of goods to safer and more profitable neighborhoods than Hare's Corner was likely to be in future. The camp was filled all day and the following night with crowds of inconsolable friends, who seemed determined to see the very last of each loved one who was about to depart, perhaps never to return.

At sunrise on the 20th tents were struck, camp-equipage was stowed in the wagons, knapsacks were packed,—and most of them were plethoric with a sort of luggage not countenanced in army regulations,—the assembly was beaten, the regiment formed, and the line of march taken up through deep mud for the town of Newport, where a train was in waiting to convey it to Baltimore. At Baltimore the regiment took the steamboat "Louisiana" for Old Point Comfort, and spent a jovial night on the waters of Chesapeake Bay.

The morning of October 21, 1861, when the command disembarked at Fort Monroe, was chilly and rendered dismal by a fine drizzle of rain (which sort of weather, by the way, continued for several days thereafter), and the regiment stood upon the wharf while Colonel Andrews went to report to General Wool. Very soon an aide was sent to conduct us to our camping-ground at Camp Hamilton, about a mile from the fort, whither we soon arrived, and all hands set to work to lay out the ground and pitch tents. Notwithstanding the inclemency of the weather, dress-parade was gone through with, much to the surprise of other regiments situated near us.

We found ourselves to be a portion of General Mansfield's brigade of General Wool's division, and were associated with the following-named regiments, viz.: Twentieth New York (German Turners), Colonel Max Weber; Sixteenth Massachusetts, Colonel Wyman; Ninety-ninth New York (Union Coast Guard), Colonel Wardrop; and Forty-eighth Pennsylvania, Colonel Nagle.

THE FIRST WINTER CAMP.

The camp-ground was low, and the long-continued rains had turned it into a marsh; but one day's work sufficed to cure the evil by draining, ditching, and elevating company tent floors and parades.

For several months following the regiment was enabled to profit by the constant exercise of every kind of field duty, guard, picket and camp, and daily drill by company, battalion, brigade, and skirmishing. During this period, also, the officers were instructed in the perplexities of morning reports, monthly and quartermaster's returns, muster-rolls, clothing-rolls, descriptive lists, etc. Strict discipline, combined with judicious instruction, through these months of preparatory schooling, made our regiment one of the best volunteer organizations in the service, and inspired each man with a just pride in it that proved a most excellent *esprit de corps* throughout its succeeding severe campaigns of marching and fighting. Colonel Andrews had secured brass shoulder-scales and white gloves for the men, required the officers to provide themselves with epaulets and the regulation felt hat and plumes, and had furnished Drum-Major Dooley with the tallest and most gorgeous of shakos, with trimmings to match. Our dress-parades had become a fine military pageant to the other regiments of the brigade, some of which changed the time for their own evening parade to a later hour that they might have the opportunity to witness ours. Frequently among the spectators that honored our parades were seen Generals Wool and Mansfield, with their staff-officers, and these commanders paid us many compliments on the appearance and discipline of the regiment and the fine military bearing of officers and men.

One day we learned that President Lincoln was at the fort and would inspect us at dress-parade. It is needless to say that every man exerted himself to make as imposing a martial appearance as possible. The adjutant's call sounded, and the companies formed for parade, the men noting with observant eyes the unusually great concourse that surrounded our regimental parade-ground. As the band was "beating off," the President, accompanied by a very large escort, all mounted, arrived upon the ground and, turning his horse's head to the right, followed directly behind the band, with his entire escort, mostly civilians, following after; but when the band had reached the left of the regimental line and had turned to the right-about to march back to its position, and Drum-Major Dooley, with his glittering staff presented at an angle of forty-five degrees from his manly breast, had advanced with martial stride through the midst of the musicians, he suddenly came face to face with the President, and all were brought to a dead halt. The situation was growing serious. There sat the President, looking somewhat embarrassed, and there stood Dooley, firm as the rock of Gibraltar; the equestrian brigade supporting the President, and the band resolutely backing up the drum-major, " marking time" and playing away with their best energy. After a few moments of hesitation, which provoked a hearty peal of laughter from all, the President finally realized that he was in the enemy's country, where martial law was supreme, and that, therefore, the civil branch of the government should give way to the military; and, doubtless, recognizing the drum-major's determination to do his duty or die in his tracks, turned out of the way with all his followers, and opened the road for Dooley and the band out of their dilemma.

The usual monotony of a winter camp did not manifest itself to any great extent in our regiment, for the energy of the men was as conspicuous in devising methods of passing the time profitably and agreeably as it was in perfecting themselves in their duties. The religious element (and it seemed to be quite large) soon organized a Soldiers' Christian Association, under the direction of Chaplain Murphey, the frequent meetings of which were numerously attended, and were conducted with spirit and fervor. This society existed in the regiment until its muster-out. For those who were more mirthfully inclined the requisite talent was found for the emergency; and to those enterprising spirits the entire division was greatly indebted for many pleasant hours. A number of the officers, under the lead of Lieutenant Oates and Lieutenant Rickards, obtained the colonel's permission to employ detachments of volunteers in cutting and hauling logs and building a theatre. In the course of a few weeks a building was completed large enough to seat four hundred persons, provided with a roomy stage, shifting scenery, a drop-curtain, appropriately painted, an orchestra inclosure, chandeliers equipped with tin sconces for candles, foot-lights, and dressing-rooms.

About the time this building was ready for occupation the Army of the Potomac had landed and gone up the Peninsula to Yorktown. The opening entertainment was a ball, given by the regiment to the officers of the fort and the camp and their wives. For this occasion the theatre was beautifully decorated with flags and evergreens, and a brilliant and distinguished company enjoyed the dancing until a late hour. Among the guests were the officers of a French war-vessel and several of General McClellan's staff-officers. Refreshments were liberally provided in the officers' mess-tent, and Lieutenant Oates distinguished himself in dispensing the hospitality of the regiment by plying the Duke de Chartres with too much eggnog.

Some of the wags amused themselves by nailing to a tree outside the picket-line a paper containing an invitation to General Magruder and staff to attend this ball; which, they said, was a polite recognition of General Magruder's attentions to us, by sending in a flag of truce regularly

once a week summoning us to surrender Fort Monroe
forthwith or remain in it at our peril.

A dramatic company was formed also, and the first per-
formance was given early in the spring, all the costumes
having been sent for to Baltimore, and some of the scenes
obtained from the Boothenian Dramatic Association of
Wilmington. The first programme presented " La Tour
de Nesle," in which Lieutenant Oates played Captain
Burridan, Corporal Norris P. Eccleston personated Queen
Marguerite, and Adjutant Seville took the part of Count
Savoisy; Lieutenant James Rickards as Gaultier d'Alnay,
Lieutenant E. C. Alexander as Sierre Roual, Lieutenant T.
B. Hizar as Enguerrand de Marigny, Lieutenant J. P. Postles
as Orsini, Captain D. S. Yardley as Jehan, Sergeant John L.
Brady as Philip d'Alnay, and Private A. Lockwood as Landri.
This was followed by a farce entitled " B. B., or the Benicia
Boy;" and between the pieces Sergeants C. S. Shaeffer and
Allen Tatem sang a duet, called " Eighty Years Ago."

The audience which assembled to honor this first rep-
resentation was, to use the well-worn phraseology of the
newspapers, a large, fashionable, and intelligent one, em-
bracing as it did all the officers of the fort and camp not
on duty, with many ladies ; and loud and earnest were the
plaudits bestowed on the enterprising members of the
Delaware Regiment for such a valuable contribution to the
amusements of camp-life. Lieutenant James Rickards won
for himself quite an enviable reputation as a comedian
in the part of Diggory in the " Spectre Bridegroom," and
in the comic rôles of other pieces. The theatre proved
quite an efficient means for the preservation of discipline

3

and strict attention to duty among those men who need
some extraneous aid to conscience to enable them to
properly acquit themselves in that respect; for, as there
was not room for more than a hundred of the non-commissioned officers and privates in the space allotted to them,
ten tickets for admission were daily placed at the disposal
of each company commander, to be given to those men
who stood highest for obedience of orders and were cleanest
on and off parade.

On the 1st of November it fell to the lot of Captain
Tanner and his company to go out on a scout to Fox Hill
Station, the extreme outpost, and to receive a flag of truce
accompanied by seven rebel officers,—they had brought
the usual summons from General Magruder "to get out."
This meeting with rebel officers proved a lively theme for
conversation among the men, and the members of Company
H were desirable acquisitions to all circles for some days
thereafter, having beheld and talked with genuine "Johnny
Rebs."

It was quite evident that the main object of this strong
delegation of rebel officers was to gain information, for they
desired to go into Hampton on the pretext of wanting to
find a colored woman; but Captain Tanner detained them
at the outpost and sent word to General Mansfield, who was
at the time near the picket-line. The general came to meet
the flag of truce, sent the rebel officers back, and commended Captain Tanner for his discretion.

Permission having been obtained from General Wool to
bring to camp boards and scantling from the burnt houses
in Hampton, details were sent out daily for this purpose,

and the quarters of officers and men were much improved in comfort. A neat frame building was erected for the adjutant's office, which, as it was also the regimental post-office, soon became the favorite lounging-place of the officers, and many a humorous story was told and many a hearty laugh was heard around the sheet-iron stove that then was the centre of attraction.

A pioneer corps was formed on the 7th of November, and for several weeks much attention was given to teaching the men the bayonet exercise and drilling them in skirmishing, which instruction rendered the regiment so efficient in this kind of service as to make it nearly certain to be called on for that duty in the later days of active campaigning.

Quite a furore of excitement was raised on the 21st of November by the arrival in camp of a messenger from Captain Watson, who had been sent out with his company scouting. It appeared that the enemy had been of the same mind, and had also despatched a scouting-party, or, rather, a reconnoissance in force, consisting of infantry, cavalry, and two guns. This was the force that Company A encountered, and at once availing themselves of their lately-acquired knowledge of skirmishing, deployed, and kept the enemy amused at long range for several hours, until word was brought to camp, and reinforcements in the shape of three companies of the Twentieth New York, under the command of no less a personage than General Mansfield himself, with about forty staff-officers, volunteers from the other regiments, came to their relief, and the enemy was bluffed.

The canvas bag for receiving the mail hung outside of Major Smyth's tent, and was under his care. For a few days, in the latter part of November, letters had been abstracted and their valuable contents, principally money, were stolen. Major Smyth set himself to discover the thief, so arranging his plans that any person coming from the outside to dishonestly tamper with the mail must inevitably be detected. A close watch was kept up for several days and no discovery made, though other letters were missed from the pouch. At length the major solved the mystery by finding that the pilferer was his own colored servant, whom he promptly sent into durance vile.

Through December and January a great deal of sickness prevailed in the camp, in the nature of fevers and diarrhœa, and Surgeon Maull took active and efficient measures to meet the emergency. A large stone mansion close to the camp was turned into a hospital and comfortably fitted up with beds and other needful furniture, and a supply of medicines was secured. The hospital was soon filled with patients, and although the sick numbered upwards of a hundred, not more than nine members of the regiment died of disease prior to the 1st of May.

About the 23d of March, Captain Neal Ward, of Company C, was missed from camp, and as he did not appear within the next day or two, it was feared that he had wandered beyond the lines and had been captured; but all suspense was set at rest on the 26th, when the body of a man was found in the water not far from the camp and identified as the remains of Captain Ward. A day or two afterwards his body was sent home to Delaware in charge of an escort from his company.

Previous to this time several changes had already oc-curred among the officers of the line. Lieutenant Francis McCloskey, of Company C, resigned November 1, 1861, and on December 20th Captain Enoch J. Smithers, of Com-pany D, tendered his resignation. On the same date First Lieutenant David S. Yardley was promoted to be captain of the latter company, Second Lieutenant William F. Smith was advanced to be first lieutenant, and Sergeant-Major James Lewis was promoted to be second lieutenant. Sergeant Joseph C. Nicholls, of Company E, was appointed sergeant-major on the same day. Second Lieutenant Eze-kiel C. Alexander, of Company H, was promoted to first lieu-tenant of Company C December 27th, and Sergeant-Major Nicholls to second lieutenant of Company H. Sergeant Charles B. Tanner, of Company H, was also made sergeant-major. March 31, 1862, First Lieutenant John R. Vanloan, of Company H, resigned.

On the 8th of March we were witnesses for the first time of an engagement with the enemy. On this occasion the battle was a naval one, in which the enemy possessed such an overwhelming advantage that, deeply interested as we were in the issue, we could not fail to be greatly depressed in spirit and wofully discouraged as to the results. About mid-day a mysterious-looking craft that resembled a huge roof came from the direction of Norfolk, and proceeded towards the " Cumberland " and " Congress," two war-ves-sels, which were anchored near together off Newport News. This, we were soon informed, was the wonderful

ironclad that we had so often heard the rebels were building at Portsmouth, and with which they threatened to
crush our men-of-war like egg-shells and capture all our
seaports, finishing with the Federal capital. It was, in
truth, the redoubtable " Merrimac." Crowding the roofs of
the houses along the shore, and other eligible points of
observation, we witnessed this marine monster ram to destruction those two noble vessels, the " Cumberland" and
the " Congress," treating with utter contempt the shower
of heavy shot that was poured against her iron ribs. This
completed the havoc of that day, for the " Minnesota" had
grounded in water too shallow to permit the " Merrimac"
to approach her with safety, so she steamed back to Norfolk triumphantly, as the shades of evening were falling on
the burning wreck of the " Congress" and the shattered
spars of the " Cumberland" projecting but a few feet above
the surface of the water, with the stars and stripes still
floating from the mast.

The night of anxiety that followed brought no rest to
the occupants of the fort and camp. It was known that a
large force was co-operating by land under the command of
General Magruder, and, as it was certain that the narrow
and flat peninsula we occupied would be utterly untenable
under the fire the enemy could bring to bear upon it from
Hampton Roads, our only alternative was to cut our way
through any force the foe might oppose to us beyond
Hampton. During the night a detachment was sent to
Newport News, under the command of Major Smyth, with
ammunition for the troops there. Towards morning our
hopes were revived by a rumor that an ironclad called the

"Monitor" had arrived to encounter the dreaded "Merrimac." At the first streak of dawn thousands of anxious eyes swept the broad expanse of water in search of the promised succor, but to our grievous disappointment nothing that bore the slightest resemblance to an ironclad capable of trying conclusions with the "Merrimac" could be descried.

About nine o'clock the "Merrimac" was seen coming down the Elizabeth River, and in due time she appeared, accompanied by the rebel sloop "Jamestown" and a steamboat loaded with excursionists from Norfolk to see the fun. The ram steered at once for the "Minnesota," which was still aground on the bar. Then we heard a muffled report, and observed a puff of white smoke afar off in the direction of Pig Point, and, on levelling our glasses upon the spot, we could make out a dark streak on the water surmounted by what seemed to be a black bandbox. The rebel ram paused in its onward rush, appeared to reconnoitre the singular craft that had the impudence and temerity to send so defiant a challenge, then opened on it vigorously, at the same time altering her course, in order to close with her mysterious antagonist. This strange specimen of naval construction at length approached near enough to enable us to observe its shape and size, and one of the facetious boys of Company F pronounced it "a cheese-box on a raft." At length the battle grew hot and furious, the "Merrimac" rushed at the "Monitor" to ram it, and her long prow passed over the "Monitor's" low deck, doing no injury; but before the ram could disengage itself from its agile foe several shots were fired under the roof of rolled iron, doing fatal execution, and one or two directly into its port-holes. When, at last, the "Merrimac" succeeded in escaping from her perilous situation, much of her appetite for gore seemed to be appeased, and she drifted away apparently, not firing a shot, while the plucky little "Monitor" followed, firing with regularity and precision. Finally, as it appeared, the monster had decided what to do, and turned her bow towards Norfolk, making off with all the speed at her command.

This action put an effectual stop to the destructive exploits of the "Merrimac" (or the "Virginia," as the rebels had named her), for as often as she appeared she ventured out no farther than was sufficient to get sight of the "Monitor," at which she would return to safe harbor.

Second Lieutenant James Rickards, of Company B, was promoted to be captain of Company C on April 1st; Second Lieutenant J. C. Nicholls, of Company H, was transferred to Company B; Sergeant-Major Charles B. Tanner was promoted to second lieutenant of Company H; First Lieutenant E. C. Alexander, of Company C, was transferred to Company H; and Sergeant David W. Gemmill, of Company I, was appointed sergeant-major.

ACTIVE OPERATIONS.

At length the time arrived when we were to have our share in active operations. Early in May, 1862, President Lincoln came to Fort Monroe, and, in conjunction with General Wool, planned an attack on Norfolk. On the 9th we received marching orders, and made preparations by cooking rations and issuing ammunition. During the night we marched quietly to the fort and embarked on steamboats and barges; and at daylight on the 10th we crossed the channel and landed at Ocean View, took up the line of march over dusty roads for Norfolk, distant seventeen miles. This proved to be a severe trial to the men, encumbered with heavy knapsacks, blankets, overcoats, and cartridge-boxes, sweltering with the heat and stifled with dust, and a large number of overcoats and blankets were left scattered by the way. A slight opposition to our progress at Tanner's Creek by the enemy was a welcome relief to the weary men, who enjoyed an hour's rest in the shade while the rebel battery that disputed our crossing was being persuaded to retire. We reached the suburbs of Norfolk in the evening, inside the formidable and well-constructed earth-works built by the enemy for the defence of the city, where Mayor Lamb and a deputation of citizens were in waiting to surrender the city.

That night our tents were pitched upon the terreplein of the rebel fortifications, our pickets were set and our camp-guard posted, and all retired to much-needed rest; but about midnight everybody was suddenly aroused by a loud explosion. The camp soon became thronged with men eager to learn the cause of the terrible report, the violence of which shook the earth. All the information that could be gathered was from the sentries on post, who said that when the explosion was heard a tall column of fire shot into the air in the direction of Craney Island. After sunrise we learned that our dreaded enemy, the " Merrimac,'' had been blown up by the rebels, and her once almost invulnerable hull now lay at the bottom of the roadstead.

Near noon on that day the army marched into Norfolk, and the First Delaware was selected to act as provost-guard in the city. The companies were quartered in several buildings, and headquarters were established in the offices of the jail. The citizens kept themselves secluded for a few days, and acted spitefully for a time, but gradually they appeared in the streets and opened their houses as they found that their fears of the Yankees were groundless, and that the hated foe were nothing of a more formidable character than well-behaved and tolerably handsome soldier boys. The practice of holding dress-parades in the public square, which was commenced about a week after the occupation, entirely broke the shyness and reserve of the citizens, who gathered in great numbers, a majority of whom were ladies, to witness our military displays and listen to the excellent music our band always furnished. Indeed, before the regiment was relieved from provost duty in Norfolk the men had grown to be great favorites with many of the citizens, and when they departed they left many sore hearts and sad faces behind them, and not a few matrimonial engagements.

During the month of July Major Smyth was provost-marshal of Portsmouth, and won many warm and substantial friends among the citizens by his manly and courteous behavior.

On the 25th of June Lieutenant Van Trump, of Company I, resigned, and Commissary-Sergeant Charles S. Schaeffer was promoted to fill the vacancy.

Colonel Andrews became quite anxious concerning the health and discipline of the regiment after several weeks' sojourn in the city. He often remarked that six months of that kind of duty would forever ruin the organization, morally as well as physically, and begged to be sent into the field. This petition General Viele and Provost-Marshal Lamson were loath to grant, as the men were orderly and obedient, the officers zealous and capable, and the citizens desired them to remain; but early in July the colonel's wishes were gratified, and the regiment was ordered to Suffolk, a small village on the Nansemond River, about twenty-five miles from Norfolk. Here we went into camp, and drilling and other hardening exercises were resumed, and the men speedily regained their former efficiency. As the location of the camp was on the border of the great Dismal Swamp, it was not long until malarial diseases began to manifest themselves among the men, and the hospital was full to overflowing throughout the following month of August. Fully three-fourths of the regiment suffered with fevers in some form or another, and this evil became so distressing that the colonel was more anxious to escape the miasma of the swamp than he was to break loose from the demoralizing effects of Norfolk.

During our stay at Suffolk a great many changes took place among the officers. On the 17th of July Second Lieutenant James Lewis, of Company D, was promoted to first lieutenant of Company C, Sergeant-Major David W. Gemmill to second lieutenant of Company K (Lieutenant Burton having gone to the Signal Corps), and Sergeant Andrew Walls, of Company C, was made sergeant-major. On the 21st Captain Charles Lespés, of Company I, resigned, and on the 23d Second Lieutenant Hugh Sweeney, of Company C, also resigned. These vacancies brought more promotions, and on the 24th First Lieutenant Thomas B. Hizar was advanced to the command of Company I, and Second Lieutenant Albert S. Phillips, of Company E, to be first lieutenant of Company I. Then Sergeant-Major Walls was promoted to be second lieutenant of Company C, and Sergeant John T. Dent, of Company G, was made sergeant-major. On August 5th Second Lieutenant Joseph C. Nicholls, of Company B, was promoted to be first lieutenant, *vice* First Lieutenant James A. Oates resigned. August 18th the regiment met with a lamentable loss in the discharge of our excellent band. In compliance with an economizing order from the War Department, we were compelled to part with Principal Musician John B. Ritchie and the following-named musicians of our band, viz.: Philip Cahill, Albert T. Hyatt, William A. Parker, John Worth, Augustus M. L. Groff, Henry Haddock, Charles H. Henderson, John Parker, James B. Walls, Charles E. Condon, Holton Yarnall, Matthew Croft, Thomas M. Hoyle, John P. Coverdale, Levi Sylvester, James T. Haddock, Richard H. B. Wisdom, John T. Yates, John H. Walls, and Joshua Hoyle. The departure of these well-beloved comrades was quickly followed by another serious loss, in the death, on the 30th of August, of First Lieutenant Benjamin E. Adams, of Company F, who had been sick for a long time in Norfolk.

Doubtless the surviving comrades of our regiment will remember the excitement in the camp at Suffolk when the news was received relative to the threatened proclamation of emancipation and the project of organizing black regiments. Some of the Hotspurs became quite indignant, and indulged in a little intemperate language ; but, to the credit of the First Delaware, it can be said that no overt act of insubordination occurred, though some were heard of in other regiments. Our men assembled together and discussed the proposition with much calmness and good sense, and reached the conclusion that the slaves ought to be freed at all events as a war measure, and that if they were, they were as good food for rebel bullets as white men, and then contentedly turned their attention to their duties.

THE BATTLE OF ANTIETAM.

The hot month of August at Suffolk was a sore trial to the men of the regiment, principally on account of the interminable succession of drills and inspections, and the monotony grew to be almost intolerable to the men who carried the muskets. Lieutenant-Colonel Hopkinson would take the command through a lively battalion drill in the morning, his favorite exercises being movements " left in front," and Major Smyth would take the regiment out for another airing in the afternoon, and give it a season of skirmish-drill or the firings, with blank and ball cartridges, and Colonel Andrews would perform his share by parading the companies for inspection. This round of duties became so wearisome to the men that they sighed for a little excitement of some kind for a variety. The excitement so much desired was not long coming. On the 6th of September General Max Weber, who commanded the brigade, received orders to proceed with his command to Washington and join the Army of the Potomac, then on its way into Maryland to repel Lee's invasion. All was bustle and activity in the camp thenceforth, and never did soldiers pack their knapsacks for a march to meet the enemy with lighter hearts or more genuine enthusiasm than did the men of the First Delaware on this occasion.

Camp was broken on the morning of the 8th of September, the command marched to the railroad and took the cars for Norfolk, where they embarked on the transport "State of Maine," and steamed up Chesapeake Bay and the Potomac River to Washington, where we arrived on the evening of the 9th, and, for want of suitable quarters, were compelled to make our beds in the streets of the city. Notwithstanding the rudeness of our couches and the lack of comforts and conveniences for making our toilets, the regiment presented a fine and imposing appearance on the morning of the 10th as it marched along Pennsylvania Avenue with full ranks, company front. We passed through Georgetown, and went into bivouac at night near the village of Rockville, Md. The line of march was resumed next morning, and for several days it continued through Urbana, Poolesville, and Frederick, arriving at Middletown on the afternoon of the 15th, having overtaken the army that led the advance. On the 16th we passed through Turner's Gap, crossing the field on which the battle was fought on the 14th, where burial-parties were still engaged in burying the dead, and passing through Boonsborough and Keedysville, we halted for the night on the west side of Antietam Creek. Here we were assigned to the Third Division, Second Corps, commanded by General W. H. French, the corps being under the command of General E. V. Sumner. The enemy lay quite close, and a lively artillery fight was going on, but, in spite of this, the commissary-train proceeded to the front and issued rations, which came none too soon for our men, who had been marching away from the supply-train for the past two days, and whose haversacks were sadly collapsed. This duty was entered upon by the men with hearty zeal, and for a time withdrew their attention entirely from the artillery practice. At this time, among the provisions taken from the wagons was a barrel of beans, upon which one of the men of our regiment took a seat. A few minutes later a shot from the enemy struck the barrel, scattering the beans, as well as the occupant of the barrel. Gathering himself up, he remarked, "If that is the way rations are issued here, I don't want any. I am not at all hungry, thank you." While this artillery duel was raging, Lieutenant James Lewis, who was acting as adjutant (Adjutant Seville having been left at Fort Monroe sick with bilious fever), while lying on the hill-side a short distance in front of the lines, was struck in the foot by a piece of shell and carried to the rear. Thus Lieutenant Lewis was the first man in the regiment who shed his blood in the war of the Rebellion.

Early on the morning of the 17th of September the troops were under arms, and brigades and regiments were moving to different parts of the field. Our regiment, with its brigade and division, crossed the creek by fording and marched about a mile, when it was halted and faced to the left. Then was heard the command, "Fix bayonets!" and every man knew that at last he was about to meet the enemy in a deadly encounter.

The line of battle pressed forward through a cornfield, under a brisk fire of batteries and small-arms, no skirmishers having been advanced. On emerging from the cornfield the line was thrown into some confusion by scaling a post-and-rail fence on the edge of the field, and being under a galling fire, was hurriedly formed while moving rapidly forward. The enemy's position was but a few rods away, and his line ran obliquely to ours, so that in the charge the right of our regiment was much nearer the enemy than the left. One line of rebels was posted in a sunken road, while across the road, on rising ground, was a second line and their batteries. The fire the enemy was thus able to bring to bear on our single line was so destructive that even veteran troops would have been repulsed. As it was, the right of the division, which approached nearest the sunken road, was staggered and recoiled, and the right of our regiment was forced back to the edge of the cornfield, while the remainder could make no farther advance. At this moment the supporting troops behind us, instead of charging through our line upon the enemy, halted in the cornfield and fired on us from the rear, thereby forcing the command to retire a few yards to avoid the fire from our supports. Here our regiment rallied and returned the enemy's fire with telling effect. On the ground, a few yards in advance, where the line was first arrested, lay a large number of our men, killed or wounded, and among them lay the colors of the regiment, one of which was held by Lieutenant-Colonel Hopkinson, who was wounded. Major Smyth, Captain Rickards, Lieutenants Postles, Tanner, and Nicholls, Sergeants Dunn and

McAllister, with several other non-commissioned officers, rallied a large number of the men for the purpose of returning to the original line, recovering the colors, and holding the position, if possible.

They sallied gallantly to the front under a terrible tornado of shot, and held the position for a considerable time, in connection with a company of the Fifth Maryland Volunteers, commanded by Captain Faehtz. While holding this front line Captain Rickards was killed. A rebel soldier was seen approaching with a limping gait, and using his musket as a support. Sergeant Dunn raised his musket, saying, " I'll drop that fellow," but before he could fire, his piece was struck down by Captain Rickards, who exclaimed, " You wouldn't shoot a wounded man !" At that instant the advancing rebel levelled his gun and shot Captain Rickards, who died a few minutes afterwards. The dastard rebel fell in his tracks, riddled with bullets.

When the regiment retired from the field both colors were brought with it, one by Lieutenant C. B. Tanner and the other by Sergeant Allen Tatem, one of the color-guard.

The bravery and self-possession of the officers and men who thus represented the First Delaware on this front line excited the admiration of the regiment, and thenceforth they were held in the highest esteem as soldiers.

When Lieutenant Lewis was wounded, Lieutenant J. P. Postles was appointed acting adjutant, and performed the duties of that position with much credit to himself and to the entire satisfaction of the colonel. Lieutenant Postles, during the battle, rode " Calico," the piebald horse belonging to Chaplain Murphey, which rendered him a conspicuous target for rebel bullets, and, though the horse was wounded, Lieutenant Postles escaped to render other distinguished services on later fields as a gallant and dashing staff-officer.

As it is important, in a sketch as brief as this must necessarily be, to preserve the official reports, which set forth the movements and events with great accuracy, the part taken by the regiment in this sanguinary action shall be told in the report of Colonel Andrews, which is as follows, viz.:

HEADQUARTERS FIRST DELAWARE INFANTRY,
THIRD BRIGADE, THIRD DIVISION, SECOND CORPS,
NEAR SHARPSBURG, MD.

CAPTAIN BURLEIGH, A.A.G., ON THE STAFF OF BRIGADIER-GENERAL MAX WEBER.

CAPTAIN,—The first Delaware Infantry, forming the right of Brigadier-General Max Weber's brigade, after fording Antietam Creek, marched in column for a mile, then facing to the left, advanced in line of battle, forming the first line of General French's division. The enemy's batteries now opened a severe fire. Having advanced steadily through woods and cornfields, driving all before us, we met the enemy in two lines of battle posted in a road, or ravine, four feet below the surface of the adjoining field, with a third line in a cornfield in the rear, the ground gradually rising, so that they were able to fire over the heads of those in the ravine; our right was also exposed to the sudden and terrible fire from the troops who succeeded in breaking the centre division of the line of battle. We were at this time about twenty paces off the enemy, and returned their fire for some time with much coolness and effect. A charge was then ordered and attempted, but our second line, composed of new levies, instead of supporting our advance, fired into our rear. We had now lost one-third of our men, and eight officers commanding companies were either killed or wounded. Under these circumstances, we fell back gradually to a stronger position, until relieved by our third line, composed of veterans, under General Kimball. This was our first battle, and I cannot speak in too high praise of the conduct of the officers and men.

The following officers, all commanding companies, were killed or wounded: Killed, Captains Watson, Leonard, and Rickards. Wounded, Captains Yardley, Woodall, and Shortledge, and Lieutenants Swiggett and Tanner. In fact, but few escaped. The color-guard were all killed or wounded; the field-officers' horses killed.

The command exhibited a degree of gallantry, efficiency, and personal bravery seldom equalled. I must also particularly mention the services of Lieutenant-Colonel Hopkinson, Major Smyth, and acting Adjutant Postles, who behaved with exemplary coolness and bravery.

JOHN W. ANDREWS,
Colonel First Delaware Infantry.

September 18, 1862.

Of the six hundred and fifty men that entered this engagement with the regiment, two hundred and eighty-six were either killed or wounded. The colonel's horse, "Spot," was killed, and some of the men used his body as a breastwork.

The names of the non-commissioned officers and privates who were killed in this action, or who died of the wounds received therein, are as follows:

Company A.—Killed, Corporal John Brierly, and Privates Thomas Haskins, Joshua Kelly, Benjamin F. Lee, John Lindsey, John McGarrity, Edward Mosely, and Eli Shepherd. Died of wounds, Privates John Crow and William Lock.

Company B.—Killed, Corporal Nelson Wood, and Privates Samuel Laughlin, William Shaw, and Bayard M. Wilson.

Company C.—Killed, Privates Manus Boyle, Sr., Hugh Connor, Daniel Duffy, Charles Igiams, Jonathan Jerels, David Lawrence, and John O'Neal. Died of wounds, Private Patrick O'Brian.

Company D.—Killed, Privates John Carlan, Hugh Connor, John George, William Lewis, and Edward Quinn. Died of wounds, Private Major G. Blades.

Company E.—Killed, Privates Minos J. Melson, John H. Smith, and Nicholas R. Watson. Died of wounds, Privates Joseph P. McColley and Samuel Mumford.

Company F.—Killed, Corporal James H. Lucas, and Privates John H. Johnson, Eben Scott, and James Simpson. Died of wounds, Privates James P. Dickson, Barnard Mc-Geehan, and Thomas A. Simpson.

Company G.—Killed, Private Thomas Senn. Died of wounds, Sergeant Philip R. Spicer, and Privates William Seville, Thomas M. Sweeney, and Charles H. Robelen.

Company H.—Killed, Privates Alexander Baxter, Wilson Meally, and John J. Walker. Died of wounds, Privates Philip Gregory and Jehu Porter.

Company I.—Killed, Private William Guthrie.

Company K.—Killed, Privates George Jerrell and Thomas Likens.

When the command was ordered to the Army of the Potomac Captain Evan S. Watson was absent on duty in Wilmington, but hastened to reach his company, and led them into action. He fell while gallantly encouraging his men in the advance. Captain James Leonard was instantly killed in the close contest near the enemy's line.

The entire color-guard were shot down, either killed or wounded, and the colors were so torn and tattered that they were never carried into another fight. With the losses in this engagement, and with seventy-three men on the sick-list, the noble regiment that made such a fine display a few days previously while passing through Washington was reduced in size to not more than four full companies.

On the 19th the regiment marched with the entire army to Harper's Ferry, and went into camp on Bolivar Heights, where the work of recuperation was begun, and where the army waited to supply deficiencies in men and material.

General Weber having been wounded, Colonel Andrews succeeded to the command of the brigade, and devoted himself zealously to repairing the losses and restoring the morale of the command.

Dr. Joseph W. McCullough was appointed assistant surgeon August 25, 1862, and on the 6th of September Second Lieutenant John W. Williams, of Company F, was promoted to be first lieutenant. On the 16th, First Lieutenant Alfred Gawthrop, of Company G, whose health had given way, resigned on surgeon's certificate of disability. Second Lieutenant John L. Sparks was advanced to first lieutenant, and Sergeant-Major John T. Dent was appointed second lieutenant of that company. At the same time, Sergeant Henry H. Darlington, of Company K, was promoted to be sergeant-major. On the 18th, First Lieutenant Nicholls was made captain of Company B, and Sergeant Henry Curry was promoted to first lieutenant, First Lieutenant Postles was advanced to the command of Company A, and Second Lieutenant Houseman raised to first lieutenant of that company. On the 21st, First Lieutenant William F. Smith, of Company D, was made captain of Company C.

The remainder of September and nearly the whole month

of October were passed in camp at Harper's Ferry, replenishing stores, recruiting the army, and improving its efficiency. On the 11th of October Adjutant Seville returned to duty, and was appointed acting assistant adjutant-general on the staff of Colonel Andrews. During all this time the picket-line of the enemy was kept in close proximity to our own, and the two armies watched each other with the utmost vigilance. At length General McClellan felt himself in a condition to resume the offensive, and on the 26th of October camp was once more broken, and the army moved into Virginia to seek another engagement with the foe. Lee retreated before us, or, rather, kept on the western side of the mountain-range, and marched parallel with us, thus causing frequent skirmishes at the several passes between Harper's Ferry and the Rappahannock.

Throughout this march the First Delaware had a liberal share of flanking and skirmishing, owing to its efficiency in that sort of service.

When the army arrived at Warrenton a halt of two days was made, for the apparent purpose of exchanging commanding generals, for, after a review of the entire army by General McClellan, he was relieved from the command on November 7th, and General Ambrose E. Burnside succeeded him. The line of march southwardly was then resumed, and terminated at Falmouth, opposite the town of Fredericksburg, on the Rappahannock River. It had been General Burnside's intention to at once attack the enemy at this point, south of the river, but the tardiness in the arrival of the bridge-trains prevented the accomplishment of his purpose, and before the army was ready to make the crossing the enemy had thrown up formidable intrenchments on a naturally strong site for defensive operations. The delay necessary to develop some other plan of campaign, and the approach of winter, gave the army a long rest in camp, and tents of all shapes and sizes, log shanties, and mud mansions sprang up in a few days, covering the country from above Falmouth for a distance of three miles along the road to Belle Plain.

On October 1st Second Lieutenant Charles B. Tanner, of Company H, was promoted to first lieutenant of Company D; on the 24th, Second Lieutenant William Ellison, of Company D, resigned; next day, Sergeant-Major Henry H. Darlington was promoted to fill the vacancy, and Sergeant John W. Eckles, of Company F, was appointed sergeant-major.

During November and part of December the army was kept constantly exercised in brigade and division drills, interspersed with frequent corps reviews, in addition to the usual picket and guard duties.

FREDERICKSBURG.

The monotony of camp-life in winter quarters was interrupted on the evening of the 10th of December, when orders were issued commanding a movement on the enemy, to commence early next morning. Accordingly, on the morning of the 11th, we strapped on our knapsacks again, and moving very slowly, with frequent halts, night found the army massed in the valley and woods bordering on the river, opposite the town of Fredericksburg. The delay in crossing was occasioned by the sharpshooters of the enemy, concealed in the buildings of Fredericksburg along the shore, opposing the construction of the bridge. A heavy cannonade was opened on these houses, and volunteers crossed the river in boats and gallantly drove the enemy from their covert, after which the engineers laid the bridge late in the afternoon. During the night, working-parties cut down the bluff near the Lacey House, to allow of the entrance to the bridge of the artillery and wagons. About sunrise on the 12th we passed over and occupied the town. The enemy was ominously silent, and, apprehending sudden attack, the roll of companies was called every hour during the day, to keep the men from wandering from the command. The night was spent in the houses of the city, nearly all of which had been deserted by their disloyal owners.

On the morning of the 13th the troops were ordered to stand to arms, and be ready to move at a minute's notice.

Just previous to the movement on Fredericksburg Colonel Andrews was again placed in command of the brigade, he having been relieved during the march from Harper's Ferry by Colonel Dwight Morris, of the Fourteenth Connecticut Volunteers, whose commission antedated that of Colonel Andrews, and the regiment was under the command of Major T. A. Smyth, Lieutenant-Colonel Hopkinson having been left on the north side of the river, disabled by sickness.

About noon the command was heard, " Fall in !" followed by " Load at will !" At this moment the First Delaware was ordered to proceed by the right flank at double-quick up a street running towards the rebel position, file to the right when the canal was crossed, face to the left at the foot of Marye's Hill, deploy as skirmishers, and lead the advance line of attack on the enemy's work. This was felt to be, in truth, the post of honor, and right nobly did the regiment respond to this call to perform such a perilous duty as to lead the van in an assault of the enemy's stronghold. This attack was made in connection with a regiment from the First Brigade, the Eighth Ohio Volunteers, and, under the command of Major Smyth, the men bravely dashed up the hill through a perfect storm of bullets, shot, and shell, to the very rifle-pits of the enemy, where they were compelled to seek such shelter as they could find, since very few men of the several divisions that followed them up that awful slope reached as advanced a position on the field as did the skirmish-line.

In this gallant charge of the skirmishers, Captain Crossley distinguished himself by his bravery and self-possession; for, above the roar and rattle of cannon and musketry, his voice could be distinctly heard, shouting, " Steady, men, steady!" and his tall form could always be seen in the front of his company line. At dark the regiment escaped from its hazardous situation and fell back to the town.

As before, we shall let the official report of Colonel Andrews tell the story of this engagement. Our revered colonel had become helpless from exposure and fatigue during the battle, though he ably commanded the brigade until its close, and was so ill that he was compelled to go home with the sick and wounded. The following is his report:

WILMINGTON, DEL., December 27, 1862.
CAPTAIN JOSEPH W. PLUME, A.A.G. FRENCH'S DIVISION.

CAPTAIN,—I have the honor to report the following as the part taken by the Third Brigade, under my command, in the attack on the enemy's works near Fredericksburg.

On the morning of the 12th of December, at 7.30, the command, following General Kimball's brigade, and advancing by the left flank, crossed the pontoon bridge and formed line of battle in the main street of Fredericksburg, the men keeping near their arms and the roll being called every hour. This evening the Fourth New York Volunteers performed picket duty. On the morning of the 13th I received marching orders from division headquarters, and formed the brigade in rear of Kimball, in the following order, in a street running parallel with Main Street: Tenth New York Volunteers, Colonel Bendix; One Hundred and Thirty-second Pennsylvania, Lieutenant-Colonel Albright; Fourth New York Volunteers, Colonel McGregor. The First Delaware Regiment being now detailed as skirmishers in advance of Kimball's brigade, and the column formed, right in front, I reported to Brigadier-General French as being ready to move, and received my final instructions. The men seemed full of enthusiasm and eager to meet the enemy. At this time Colonel Bendix received a shell wound, and Captain Salmon Winchester assumed command of the Tenth New York Volunteers.

At 12 A.M. the command, "Forward!" was given. My instructions were to move by the flank to the position indicated, face to the front, thus forming the brigade in line of battle, and keeping one hundred and fifty paces in the rear of Kimball, to support him. We accordingly advanced briskly, under a heavy artillery fire, until we reached the position indicated, then, facing to the front, marched steadily up the slope and took a position in Kimball's rear. We remained here a short time, until finding that his ranks had become reduced, and that, although he held his ground nobly, he was unable to improve his position, I ordered my men forward to support him. The commanders of regiments led on their men in a manner worthy of all praise, and remained engaged until relieved, in turn, by the next advancing brigade. They then retired and were reformed, in the second street from the river, under their regimental commanders. Having myself become disabled during the action, I did not leave the field, and finding myself, on my return, unable to perform duty, I turned over the command to Lieutenant-Colonel Marshall,

Tenth New York Volunteers, who had been detailed on special duty on the other side of the river, with the pioneers, and was not present in the action.

In conclusion, I beg leave to state that the officers behaved with exemplary coolness, and the men with the steadiness and courage of veterans. I wish, also, particularly to mention the efficient services of Colonel John D. Mc-Gregor, Fourth New York Volunteers, wounded in the arm; Lieutenant-Colonel Charles Albright, One Hundred and Thirty-second Pennsylvania; Lieutenant-Colonel William Jameson, Fourth New York Volunteers; Major Thomas A. Smyth, First Delaware Volunteers; Major Charles Kruger, Fourth New York Volunteers; and Captain Salmon Winchester, an accomplished gentleman and a true soldier, who fell mortally wounded while commanding and leading on his regiment, the Tenth New York Volunteers· Also, to the valuable aid afforded me by the gentlemen of my staff, Lieutenant William P. Seville, A.A.G.; Lieutenant Theodore Rogers, A.D.C., severely wounded by my side while the command was under a heavy fire of musketry; and Lieutenant William C. Inhoff, A.D.C.

Having already testified to the good conduct of those under my immediate command, it becomes my duty also to state that the First Delaware Regiment, detached as skirmishers, were reported as having behaved with great courage and endurance; that, after driving the enemy's skirmishers, they sustained alone their fire for a considerable time before the supporting column arrived, and, after spending all their ammunition, they retired in good order. Major T. A. Smyth, in command, is represented as having displayed much coolness and ability. The list of casualties will be reported by Lieutenant-Colonel Marshall, now in command.

Very respectfully,

Your obedient servant,

JOHN W. ANDREWS,
Colonel Commanding Third Brigade.

Lieutenant-Colonel John W. Marshall, who succeeded to the command of the brigade immediately after the close of the battle, in his official report, thus alludes to the conduct of the First Delaware:

"The several regiments of my brigade stood up to their work nobly. The

First Regiment, Delaware Volunteers, deserves particular mention for the manner in which, as skirmishers, it opened the engagement, and remained on the field until every cartridge was expended."

He also reported the casualties in the First Delaware as ten killed, seventy-four wounded, and nine missing; but the muster-out rolls report that seventeen members of the regiment were killed at Fredericksburg, and that five others died of wounds received there, as follows: Killed, Lieutenant Henry H. Darlington, of Company D; Corporal Samuel Weir, Company A; Privates William Smith and Thomas Sinnox, Company B; Privates Manus Boyle, Jr., and William Henry Beggs, Company C; Private John C. Abel, Company D; Private John C. Carey, Company E; Corporal George W. Reice and Private John Cline, Company G; Sergeant George C. Semple, Musician Robert Long, and Private John Miller, Company H; Privates John P. Money and George Sneider, Company I; and Privates Frederick B. Ennis and Thomas Holmes, of Company K. Those who died subsequently of wounds were First Lieutenant Albert S. Phillips, Company I; Sergeant Henry H. Higgins, Company G; Corporal Lemuel J. Green and Private Napoleon Adams, Company E; and Private Robertson W. Plummer, Company D.

One other officer was wounded in this assault,—Captain William F. Smith, of Company C.

After retiring from the field at dark, the regiment was reassembled in a street next to the river, and the rolls were called to ascertain who were killed, wounded, or missing. The men were then dismissed, with the injunction to remain near the stacks of arms ready to fall in at call, as an attack was expected during the night. But the enemy made no more serious demonstration than that of throwing an occasional shell into the town. About ten o'clock the ammunition-train crossed over and our cartridge-boxes were replenished. The next day was Sunday, which we spent in caring for the wounded and repairing the damages of the previous day. At night we were ordered to recross the river with all possible silence, and the last man was out of the town before daylight on the 15th, and the various divisions were on their way to their former camping-grounds.

We were scarcely settled in our old quarters before very cold weather set in, and we comforted ourselves with the reflection that no more movements could be made until the return of spring.

On December 14th Lieutenant-Colonel Oliver P. Hopkinson resigned on account of ill health, and the command of the regiment fell to Major Thomas A. Smyth, who was promoted to the vacancy on the 18th. On the same day Sergeant-Major John W. Eckles was made second lieutenant of Company D, Sergeant Samuel A. McAllister, of Company F, was appointed sergeant-major, and on the 24th he was further promoted to be second lieutenant of Company B, and Sergeant John L. Brady, of Company C, advanced to be sergeant-major, while Captain Daniel Woodall, of Company F, was promoted to be major. On the 26th, Second Lieutenant Eckles was raised to first lieutenant of Company F; on the 28th, Second Lieutenant Charles S. Schaeffer, of Company I, was promoted to be first lieutenant of Company K; on the 30th, First Lieutenant

John W. Williams, of Company F, died of disease, and next day, First Lieutenant Franklin Houseman, of Company A, resigned.

Not long did we enjoy the rest and relaxation of our winter quarters, for early in January, General Burnside having formed another plan for a campaign, the usual order to hold ourselves in readiness to march at a moment's notice was received, and next day the army began to pass through our camp towards the upper fords. A steady rain set in soon after the movement commenced, and, as but one road could be used without exposure of the enterprise to the enemy, by the time night arrived the artillery and wagons were hopelessly mired, and the campaign was abandoned. This flurry did not affect us, for, as the Second Corps, which was to have acted as rear-guard, lay on the right of the army, we should not have broken camp until the entire army had gone by. On the 24th of January General Burnside was relieved from the chief command at his own request, and General Joseph Hooker was appointed in his stead. General Hooker at once set to work to improve the condition of the army; he instituted a few welcome changes in the rations, granted short leaves of absence, and reorganized the cavalry. During our encampment here a curious sort of intimacy sprang up between the men of the opposing armies. The river was fordable at several places above Falmouth, and the pickets were stationed on each shore, the distance across the stream being so short that conversation was carried on with ease. One day, after the battle of Fredericksburg, a rebel called out to one of our picket-guard, " Say, Yank, when are you all goin' to come over agin?" "Don't know," answered the Union picket. "Pretty soon, I guess." "You 'uns 'll never git to Richmond; d'ye know why?" asked the rebel. "No, why?" "Because you 'uns 'll have two big Hills to git over, a Longstreet to go through, and a Stonewall to cross," was the reply.

Every day exchanges of tobacco and other articles were made by the pickets, until, at length, the men used to visit each other, play cards, and pass newspapers back and forth, which having been discovered by General French, a sudden stop was put to these civilities.

In the first four months of 1863 many changes took place among the officers of the regiment. January 3d Commissary-Sergeant Edwin H. Byran was made second lieutenant of Company A; on the 6th, Sergeant-Major John L. Brady was made second lieutenant of Company D, and Sergeant Allen Tatem, of Company B, was appointed sergeant-major; on the 14th, First Lieutenant Albert S. Phillips died of his wound in the head; on the 17th, Captain Thomas Crossley, Company K, resigned on account of disability; First Lieutenant William C. Inhoff, Company K, was made captain, and next day he resigned from disability. First Lieutenant William Y. Swiggett, Company E, was promoted to captain of Company F; on the 19th, Dr. Samuel Marshall, assistant surgeon, resigned because of disability; on the 20th, Second Lieutenant Samuel A. McAllister, Company B, was made first lieutenant Company F; First Lieutenant John W. Eckles, Company F, was transferred to Company I; Sergeant J. Hart, of Company F, was made second lieutenant of that company; Sergeant-Major Allen

Tatem was advanced to second lieutenant Company H; and Sergeant James D. Simpson, Company F, was appointed sergeant-major. On February 6th Colonel John W. Andrews resigned on account of disability; on the 7th, Second Lieutenant Martin W. B. Ellegood, Company H, was promoted to captain Company E, and Second Lieutenant John L. Brady, Company D, was advanced to first lieutenant of the same company; on the 8th, Sergeant-Major Simpson was made second lieutenant Company D, and Sergeant Benjamin Y. Draper, of Company D, was appointed sergeant-major; on the 9th, Second Lieutenant Andrew Walls, Company C, was made first lieutenant Company I; on the 18th, our prize drum-major, Patrick Dooley, was swept away by the general order to muster out that regimental ornament; on the 20th, First Lieutenant John L. Sparks, of Company G, was made captain of Company K; Second Lieutenant John T. Dent was promoted to first lieutenant; Sergeant Charles W. Davis, Company D, was made second lieutenant Company G; and Sergeant Aquila M. Hizar, first lieutenant of Company K; Lieutenant-Colonel Thomas A. Smyth was advanced to the command of the regiment on the 23d, and Captain Edward P. Harris, of Company E, was elected lieutenant-colonel.

March 1st our quartermaster, Thomas Y. England, a very courteous and efficient officer, was promoted to be commissary of subsistence, with the rank of captain, and on the next day Second Lieutenant Edwin H. Bryan, of Company A, was raised to the grade of first lieutenant, and appointed regimental quartermaster; and Sergeant William Smith, of Company A, was made second lieutenant of that company; on the 3d, Captain John B. Tanner, of Company H, resigned on account of disability, and First Lieutenant Ezekiel C. Alexander became captain of the company; on the 11th, Sergeant-Major Benjamin Y. Draper was made second lieutenant of Company D, and Sergeant John W. Barney, of Company F, was appointed sergeant-major; Second Lieutenant William Smith, Company A, was made first lieutenant, and Sergeant G. T. Price, Company G, was promoted to second lieutenant Company A.

CHANCELLORSVILLE.

The men were once more growing somewhat weary of the monotonous round of duties incident to life in camp, when, on the 27th of April, the order for another movement was received. On the morning of the 28th we marched about three miles up the Rappahannock, and were set to work making roads and throwing up a small battery, the latter, probably, to deceive the enemy as to our real intentions. Next day we moved on a few miles farther and again encamped; and on the 30th we took the road again, and halted at United States Ford, where we remained till nearly sunset. As the shadows were lengthening we once more started forward, crossed the bridge, and then marched down the river until midnight, when we were halted, massed in the fields, and dropped upon the ground to sleep just where we stopped.

The battle opened early next morning, May 1st, by a desperate attack on the left of our army posted near the Chancellor House, and towards noon we were ordered to proceed in that direction. We had gone about a mile in the direction of Todd's Tavern when our orders were countermanded, and we hurried back to our former position. The enemy had occupied in strong force the range of hills we had started out to take. Having reached the spot where we had spent the previous night, our little brigade (the First Delaware and One Hundred and Thirty-second Pennsylvania) was instructed to act in support of the line in the wood on our front.

On the morning of the 2d a dropping fire, interspersed now and then with a few volleys, was carried on during the morning until about ten o'clock, at which time the enemy made a vigorous attack on our centre, and was repulsed. Late in the afternoon Stonewall Jackson's corps turned the right flank of the Eleventh Corps and completely routed it. Our brigade, leaving our knapsacks, overcoats, and blankets, was hurried forward to check the retreat of the Eleventh Corps. This we did by arresting their flight, forming them into companies, and sending them to the rear. Having accomplished this, we were countermarched in some haste back to our old bivouac to uncover Ames' battery, which was planted ready to welcome Jackson's men if they should break through the Third Corps. The close proximity of the hostile lines, and the nervousness of the men in the front of each, caused a rapid succession of volleys, cannonades, and scattering shots throughout the whole night, calling the troops into line every hour, and seriously interrupting our rest.

At daylight on the morning of the 3d the contest began in grand earnest on our front, and soon extended all along the line. About noon our little brigade was again ordered to advance and "hold the enemy." That was our mission, and we moved in without delay, drove the rebels to the plank road, and, finding ourselves in advance of our line, and connections broken on each flank, we fell back, when the firing had ceased, to our former position. The enemy, thinking our retrograde movement a retreat, made another furious charge, this time enveloping our right flank, which was held by the First Delaware. The cry at once arose, "We are outflanked!" The situation was a critical one, but was speedily rectified by the presence of mind of Colonel Smyth, who commanded a change of front to the rear on the tenth company. This order was executed in fine style by the regiment, thus facing the foe, who were quickly repulsed, and we were left in possession of the wood. Our situation was rendered more hazardous at this time by our own batteries opening on the wood we occupied, thinking, doubtless, that we were all captured. This fire from our own guns determined Colonel Albright, who commanded the brigade, to leave the wood and retire to our original line. The men were cautioned to move slowly to the rear, and when outside of the wood to reform the line left in front. This was done, and our appearance in the field, with our colors flying, caused a cessation of the fire from our batteries. The line formed, the command "About face!" was given, and at the words "Forward, march!" we moved forward in ordinary quick time, and with almost as much precision as if on review. This sudden appearance and deliberate retreat so greatly amazed our commanders, who were looking on, that a staff-officer was sent galloping towards us to learn who we were, and report in time to sweep us out of existence if we should prove to be enemies carrying the national flag. "Who commands these troops?" demanded the officer. "I do," replied Colonel Albright. "What troops are they?" asked the officer. "First Delaware and One Hundred and Thirty-second Pennsylvania, Third Brigade, Third Division, Second Corps!" was the reply, and away sped the officer with his report, which seemed to create some excitement and a little merriment among the group of generals when he reported to General Couch. "Why, general," said General Couch to General French, "that is one of your brigades." General Howard remarked to General French that we made the laziest retreat he ever saw.

The part taken by the Second Corps and its subdivisions in this battle has not been faithfully set forth in official reports and in history generally, for the reason that the corps was so scattered that the operations of its divisions and brigades were merged in those of the larger bodies they acted with. The First Division fought, most of the time, away on the left; the Second Division remained at Falmouth to support General Sedgwick. One regiment of our brigade (the Fourth New York Volunteers) was detached as a hospital guard, and the other brigades of our division were supporting the main line on our left-centre. General French, who commanded our division, was ill part of the time, and when General Hooker was disabled by the shock occasioned by a shell striking a pillar of the Chancellor House piazza, against which he was leaning, the command of the army fell to General Darius N. Couch, who was our corps commander. Thus it happened that the part taken by our brigade and regiment in this action was not fully described in the official reports of any general or acting general officers excepting that made by Colonel Albright, which will be given entire, following those of Colonel Smyth and Lieutenant-Colonel Harris. The following is the official report of Colonel Smyth:

OFFICIAL REPORTS OF CHANCELLORSVILLE.

HEADQUARTERS FIRST REGIMENT, DELAWARE VOLUNTEERS,
May 7, 1863.

LIEUTENANT W. P. SEVILLE, A.A.A.G. Third Brigade, Third Division.

SIR,—I have the honor to report that, in obedience to General Orders, No. 37, from headquarters Third Division, Second Corps, the regiment under my command marched from its camp near Falmouth at sunrise on the morning of the 28th of April, having position in the centre of the Third Brigade. We moved up the road toward Bank's Ford, near which place we halted at 11 o'clock A.M., and bivouacked for the remainder of the day and night. At 2 P.M. on the following day the march was again resumed, and we halted for the night about two and a half miles from United States Ford. On the morning of the next day the march was resumed, and crossing the Rappahannock early in the evening at United States Ford, we moved up the road to Chancellorsville, halting within a mile of that place about 11 P.M. On the 1st of May the regiment remained in column, under arms, without moving. On the morning of the 2d the enemy began shelling our position, but without effect. Late in the afternoon the regiment was formed in line of battle, facing the right. About six o'clock in the evening, the Eleventh Army Corps having given way on the right, the regiment was moved to the left of the Chancellorsville road, four companies being thrown across the road to aid in arresting the stragglers.

After the panic had somewhat abated, we received orders from Major Norval to support Captain Frank's battery, posted in the open field to the right of the headquarters of General French, one company, under the command of Captain Smith, being thrown forward to the edge of the woods as a picket-guard, where they remained during the night. On the morning of the 3d we were moved, by an order from General French, a short distance to the left, ready to advance to the support of the First Brigade, then moving to reinforce the Third Corps, heavily engaged with the enemy in front. While in this position a temporary breastwork, formed of knapsacks, fence-rails, and bags of earth, was erected as a protection against the fire of the enemy's infantry. About 7 A.M. the Third Corps, being hard pressed in front, gave way, and, in company with the One Hundred and Thirty-second Pennsylvania Volunteers, we advanced to the edge of the woods, when we encountered the enemy in considerable force, and drove him for a distance of half a mile. Then, the enemy having been reinforced, we halted, and held him in check for about three hours, when the brigade on our right gave way, allowing the enemy to gain a position on our right flank and rear. Being thus exposed to a galling fire from three directions, the regiment changed front to the rear on the tenth company, in perfect order, and, assisted with the fire from one of the batteries, repulsed the enemy, when, having received orders to retreat, we fell back in good order, and took our position in the rear of the First Brigade. The enemy having range of our position, opened upon us with shell, upon which we retired, in obedience to orders, into the woods. Having rested for about half an hour, we were ordered to the front to support the First Brigade. Taking a position in the second line of battle, we remained there, frequently exposed to a hot fire of shell and musketry, until three o'clock on the morning of the 6th, when we took up our line of march for the river, marching left in front, and following the One Hundred and Thirty-second Pennsylvania Volunteers. Without halting, we crossed the pontoon bridge at United States Ford, and reached our old camp about noon.

Our loss in the five days, during which time we were exposed to the fire of the enemy, was six killed, thirty-three wounded, and ten missing. Among the wounded is Major Woodall.

The conduct of the regiment, both officers and men, is worthy of all praise. The men who fought so bravely at Antietam and Fredericksburg forgot not their record, nor failed to add to it another page inscribed with glorious deeds of patriotic valor. Where all acted so nobly it would, perhaps, be invidious to mention any one particularly, yet the coolness under fire evinced by Lieutenant-Colonel Harris, Major Woodall, and Acting Adjutant Tanner, and the bravery of Captains Smith, Yardley, Hizar, Sparks, and Lieutenant Draper, as shown not only at the battle of Chancellorsville, but in previous engagements, entitle them to especial notice. Particularly would I call the attention of the colonel commanding to the gallant conduct of Captain Smith; always brave, at the battle of Chancellorsville his bravery was more than usually conspicuous. By his example he encouraged the men, and by his coolness aided materially in repulsing the enemy upon our flank.   Very respectfully, your obedient servant,

THOMAS A. SMYTH,
Colonel Commanding First Regiment, Delaware Volunteers.

Immediately after the return to camp the command of the brigade devolved upon Colonel Smyth, by the muster out of service of the regiments commanded by Colonels Albright and McGregor; and an order having been issued that regimental commanders should forward a list of the names of non-commissioned officers and privates whose behavior under fire was deserving of praise, the subjoined report was rendered by Lieutenant-Colonel Harris:

HEADQUARTERS FIRST DELAWARE REGIMENT,
May 27, 1863.

LIEUTENANT WILLIAM P. SEVILLE, A.A.A.G.

SIR,—I have the honor to make the following report of enlisted men in this command, according to General Order No. 53, paragraph one, as reported by their commanding officers:

Corporal William Anderson and Private Joshua Green, of Company C. The latter was wounded at the battle of Chancellorsville, both having been in all the battles in which the regiment was engaged. They have always behaved well, but more particularly in the battle of Chancellorsville, by volunteering to go to the front and find the enemy's position, which they did successfully.

Sergeant William Birney, Corporal William Murphey, and Private George F. Jones, of Company D, all behaved with the utmost coolness and bravery, thereby showing a good example to their comrades and the regiment in general. These three behaved very well in all former engagements in which the regiment was. Corporal Murphey was not in Fredericksburg. Sergeant

Birney was wounded at Fredericksburg in the foot.   Private Richard Cox, of Company H, has behaved well in all the battles in which the regiment was engaged.   He deserves particular notice for his volunteering and accompanying Corporal Anderson and Private Green, of Company C; to the front.

First Sergeant David Challenger, Sergeants William D. Birch and Henry G. Cavanaugh, Corporal Jacob H. Thompson, Privates Robert Wright, Benjamin Derity, Andrew Wilkinson, and Gardner Sands, of Company I, all deserve special notice for their bravery and coolness under fire.   Sergeant Challenger was in Antietam and Chancellorsville; Sergeants Cavanaugh and Birch were in all the battles in which the regiment was engaged.   Corporal Thompson was in Fredericksburg and Chancellorsville.   Privates Wright, Derity, and Wilkinson were through all engagements with the regiment. Wright and Wilkinson were wounded at Fredericksburg; also Gardner Sands was in all engagements.   The above-named members of Company I all did their duty, and showed great coolness and bravery, thereby encouraging all near them to stand fast.   They have behaved so in all engagements, and all deserve special notice.

Corporal D. G. Smith, of Company D, deserves great credit for the example he showed in all the engagements the regiment has been in; was wounded at Chancellorsville in the breast.

Sergeant Charles J. Steel, Corporals William C. Joseph and Robert F. Burrows, and Private Peter W. Vincent, of Company E, all deserve special notice for their daring, bravery, and coolness in the battles in which the regiment has been engaged.

Corporals James H. Barbour, Isaac P. Nickson, and Charles B. Parry, and Orderly Sergeant William H. Ferguson, of Company K, all deserve special notice for the good example they showed to their company in the different actions in which the regiment has been engaged.

First Sergeant Matthew Rodgers, Privates William B. Murry, James Simpson, and Bernard Morris, of Company B, deserve special notice for their good conduct in different engagements; they have always been conspicuous; also Private Martin Daily, who went on the field and brought several wounded off after the regiment had been ordered off.   Privates James Gamble, Joseph Schaffner, and Jacob Schaffner deserve to be mentioned, for encouraging the men to never run by their example, and while so doing were all killed.

Corporal Henry Roberts and Private Isaac Scott, of Company F, deserve great credit for their bravery at Antietam and Chancellorsville, both having been wounded by so doing in each battle.

First Sergeant William Caywood, Sergeant William Warren, and Corporals William Hanson and Adam Kinsler, of Company A, deserve great credit for their daring bravery, thereby encouraging the men to remain fast and keep cool. They have been in all the engagements in which the regiment has.

Sergeant William K. McClurg, of Company H, should also be mentioned for his good conduct; he was wounded at Chancellorsville while encouraging his men to do their duty.

Corporal Samuel L. McElwee, of Company K, deserves great credit for his heroism in all the engagements he was in; he was one of the bravest men of this command, and was killed at Chancellorsville.

I remain, very respectfully,

Your obedient servant,

E. P. HARRIS,
Lieutenant-Colonel Commanding Regiment.

In order to preserve as full an official account of this action in which the First Delaware rendered such valuable service and won merited distinction, the report of Colonel Charles Albright, who commanded the brigade, is added:

HEADQUARTERS THIRD BRIGADE, THIRD DIVISION,
May 7, 1863.

MAJOR J. M. NORVELL,

ASSISTANT ADJUTANT-GENERAL THIRD DIVISION, SECOND CORPS.

MAJOR,—I have the honor to make the following official report of the part taken by this brigade in the series of actions which occurred in the vicinity of Chancellorsville from the 1st to the 6th of May, 1863, inclusive.

On the evening of April 27th an order was received to be in readiness to march at an early hour the next day. Everything was prepared and the wagons packed before daylight. On the evening of the 28th an order was received from Major-General French commanding the division to march to the Falmouth road, which was executed. The brigade remained bivouacked on an opening in the wood, about four and a half miles from Falmouth, until 2 P.M. on the 29th, when the march was resumed, and the troops halted for the night near Bank's Ford. On the morning of the 30th, at nine o'clock, we took up the line of march for United States Ford, where the brigade crossed at 7 P.M., and continued the march to near Chancellorsville, where it arrived at twelve, midnight.

On the morning of May 1st an order was received from General French for the brigade to fall in under arms. The Fourth Regiment, New York Volunteers, was here assigned to special duty as a guard to the corps hospital located at this spot. The brigade, which then comprised the First Regiment, Delaware Volunteers, and the One Hundred and Thirty-second Regiment, Pennsylvania Volunteers, was marched half a mile on the road to Chancellorsville and halted. An order was received through Lieutenant Russell, A.D.C., to fall in, and when the column started to follow, keeping the right-hand side of the road. When the brigade started, an order was given by Lieutenant Burt, A.D.C. to General Couch, not to move until a battery was brought in front. About 11 A.M. an order came through Lieutenant Russell, A.D.C., to move forward, which we did, keeping on the plank road to Chancellorsville. Having passed the cross-road about two hundred yards, an order arrived to return in double-quick time and retire to our former camp at the hospital. On the evening of the 1st we were under arms during several attacks upon our lines. During the attack on our centre, on Saturday evening, May 2d, the brigade was formed near and facing the wood. Directions were received through Lieutenant Torbert, A.D.C., to move more to the right and rear, and subsequently to move far enough to the rear to unmask Ames' battery. Finally it was again moved, by Major Norvell, A.A.G., across the road, and I was directed to support Colonel Carroll. The brigade here intercepted all stragglers, and sent them to rejoin their respective corps. Colonel John D. MacGregor, Fourth New York Volunteers, who had so ably commanded the brigade, was compelled to retire early in the afternoon, being too ill to perform duty, and the command devolved upon me. Vigorous assaults were made by the enemy on our centre at 10.20 P.M., 11.35 P.M., and 1.15 A.M. At every attack the brigade was promptly under arms. At 5.25 A.M. on the 3d the brigade was under arms, another attack having been made on the centre. The brigade was moved by an order through Major Norvell, A.A.G., to the edge of the wood. I reached the skirt of the wood and gave the order to commence firing, as the enemy had charged, and were then in sight. The brigade delivered a well-sustained fire, and I then gave the order

to advance. The brigade moved rapidly in good order, driving the enemy
before them in great confusion, and cheered most lustily. My men captured
a good number of prisoners, whom I sent to the rear by themselves, so as not
to lessen my effective force. I kept my men well together, presenting a close
line. The men were quite cool, and obeyed every order with enthusiasm and
alacrity. In advancing through the wood I tried to keep up communication
with the First Brigade, commanded by Colonel Carroll, and General Tyler's
brigade, on my right, and threw out a number of skirmishers to feel the
ground in my immediate front, to prevent any surprise. A number of the
enemy were found concealed behind bushes, and, in some instances, fired from
trees ; placed there, doubtless, to pick off our officers. I continued to advance
cautiously in this manner, driving the enemy before me, until I found my
communications broken on both my right and left. I then deemed it prudent
to retire until I could make a union with the other lines. I accordingly fell
back about one hundred yards and took position. A furious charge was
then made on our line, and I directed the men to hold their fire until the
enemy came in sight, and then to let every shot tell. The brigade received
this assault and checked the enemy. While the men of my command were
repelling this attack the batteries in our rear were throwing shells, which ex-
ploded directly over my line. As the enemy were repulsed, and no troops
could be seen on either my right or left, I gave the word to retire, fearing
that my command might be outflanked, which, indeed, came very near oc-
curring. The enemy appeared on the right of my command, but they were
prevented from turning our rear by the timely precaution of Colonel Smyth,
of the First Delaware, who changed front to the rear on his tenth company.
I was careful that this was done without confusion, and, crossing the plain
between the wood and hospital, again occupied the line formerly held by
my command where the men's knapsacks were left. The brigade was no
sooner on this line than I was directed by an officer to move my command
by the right flank at double-quick to unmask the batteries, as they were
about to open. I marched the command across the road, and took position as
directed by General French, through Major Norvell, A.A.G., with orders to
construct rifle-pits. Before this could be commenced, however, the enemy's
batteries opened upon us with shell, wounding Major Daniel Woodall, First
Delaware, and a few men. I received an order then to march my command into the wood on my right, where it was assigned a position to sup-

port Colonel Carroll, commanding the First Brigade. I at once had the roll called and casualties ascertained. I received an order to fill up to the usual amount of ammunition, and sent details to draw the required ammunition. On the evening of the 4th an attack was made upon our line, and our position in the wood shelled. I had the command immediately under arms, and the men sustained the fire with great fortitude. Captain Hall, One Hundred and Thirty-second Pennsylvania Volunteers, and three men of my command were wounded by this fire. On the morning of the 5th the enemy made another attack on our front of the line. As the command was exposed to a fire of musketry without the satisfaction of returning it, I directed the men to collect the scattered logs and lay them in front, and, after the action was over, had it turned into a breastwork. At 8 P.M. on the 5th I received an order to prepare the brigade to march at 10 P.M., without noise. At the appointed time my command was in line and ready to move. At 3 A.M. on the 6th the command marched to the United States Ford and recrossed the bridge, and 7 o'clock P.M. found the brigade on its old campground, rectifying the confusion occasioned by the week's active service.

The losses of the brigade were as follows: First Regiment, Delaware Volunteers, five men killed, one commissioned officer and thirty-nine men wounded, and eleven men missing; total, fifty-six. One Hundred and Thirty-second Pennsylvania Volunteers, two commissioned officers wounded, two men killed, thirty-nine wounded, and one man missing; total, forty-three; aggregate, ninety-nine.

The conduct of both the First Delaware and One Hundred and Thirty-second Pennsylvania Regiments was splendid, and too much credit cannot be bestowed upon the officers and men for their gallant conduct displayed in this action. I cannot close this report without thanking Lieutenant William P. Seville, Assistant Adjutant-General; Captain H. F. Chew, Acting Assistant Inspector-General; and Lieutenant D. R. Mellick, Aide-de-Camp, for their very efficient and able services. I wish, particularly, to call your attention to Lieutenant Seville; he is an excellent officer, brave and cool in danger, and I earnestly recommend him for promotion.

I am, very respectfully,

Your obedient servant,

CHARLES ALBRIGHT,

Colonel One Hundred and Thirty-second Pa. Vols., Commanding Brigade.

The muster-out rolls show that the number of men killed at Chancellorsville was nine; four more than Colonel Albright reports, and three more than the number stated by Colonel Smyth. The following are their names: Corporal Samuel L. McElwee, Company K; Privates James Gamble and Joseph Schaffner, Company B; George H. Howard, John Poore, and Erasmuth Wolfe, Company D; William D. Vaughan, Company E; Richard W. Fisher, Company G; and John Dougherty, Company H.

Having once more reoccupied our old camp and quarters, the work of reorganization and invigoration was recommenced that the army might be ready for the field at the earliest day possible, as the season for activity was then at hand, and the enemy was so little crippled by the late contest that aggressive measures on his part were expected within the month of May.

On the 7th of May the Third Brigade was broken up by the discharge of the Fourth New York and One Hundred and Thirty-second Pennsylvania Regiments, and the First Delaware was assigned to the Second Brigade, of which Colonel Smyth became the commander.

Dr. Frederick J. Owens was appointed assistant surgeon May 8th; Second Lieutenant David Gemmill, of Company E, was dismissed on the 15th of May, and on the 20th, First Lieutenant Henry Curry, of Company B, resigned.

THE BATTLE OF GETTYSBURG.

About the middle of June a startling rumor became current throughout the army that General Lee had marched a few days previously up the valley, and that Washington was his objective-point. We surmised that our camp duties and amusements would suddenly be interrupted, and so it proved, for on the 13th the order for marching was received, and at the same time we heard that the rebels had not secured much of a lead, for a portion of our army had started after them on the 12th, and that the Second Corps was designated as the rear-guard.

The command spent all next day wandering aimlessly about the devastated camp, fully equipped for marching at a moment's warning. At 9 P.M. our share in the great movement began, and the troops filed out on the road and turned their faces northward. Several long halts in the first five miles of the route gave an opportunity to a detachment of the regiment which had been on picket the night before to overtake the command. Sunrise found us at Stafford Court-House, the enemy close at hand and apparently in a pugnacious mood. An advantageous position was chosen and line of battle formed, but, as the enemy did not seem disposed to attack, the line of march was resumed. On the 16th the corps was halted at Dumfries to replenish the haversacks, after which the route was taken, and the command went into bivouac at night on the Occoquan Creek. This march proved very exhausting, owing to the intense heat, the long-continued drouth, and the suffocating dust. The energies of the men gave way before noon each day under this accumulation of evils, and the army of stragglers brought into camp every night by the provost-guard seemed larger than the part that limped in with the colors and heard the most cheerful of all the commands laid down in the tactics : " Break ranks, march !" We passed through Fairfax Station, Centreville, over the battle-field of Bull Run, and went into camp at Gainesville, where we lay four days to recruit strength and repair damages. Then the route was resumed, and the command marched through Sudley Springs and Gum Springs, and arrived at Edwards' Ferry on the Potomac on the 26th of June. After crossing, the line of march lay through Poolesville, Barnes-ville, Urbana, and Frederick City. At this point, General Hooker was relieved from the command of the army and General George G. Meade became our chief. On Monday, the 29th, the column took to the road at 8 A.M., and passed through Mount Pleasant, Liberty, Johnstown, Union Bridge, Middletown, and finally halted late at night at Uniontown, having marched thirty-two miles. Long before night fell most of the troops were fagged out and kept moving only under great suffering. They were informed that it was regarded as of the utmost importance that the command should reach Uniontown that night, and the men endured their hardships with commendable fortitude. At one time, near the close of this memorable march, the column was halted for a brief rest, and as a general and his staff passed by, one of the men called out, "Oh, don't stop! Get fresh horses and let's go ahead. We are not tired." This was greeted by laughter loud and long, in which the general joined. After this, whenever the column halted, many voices would shout, "Why don't you get fresh horses?" But the long march came to an end, and when the command "Break ranks!" was heard, the worn-out men dropped down where they halted, wholly indifferent to the usual refreshment (a cup of hot coffee), and slept till morning. This was not generally the case with the Delaware men. It was remarked, with much surprise, that while nearly all the men were asleep the First Delaware men were scouting after wood and provisions, and that lusty camp-fires were blazing among them until after midnight. The regiment was also complimented at the close of this march for their hardiness and power of endurance, because, among the immense force of stragglers gathered up that day, very few were members of the First Delaware.

The command remained in bivouac all day on the 30th, and marched at 7 A.M. on the 1st of July about six miles, to Taneytown, where a halt was made until near noon, at which time an aide brought orders to hasten forward, as General Reynolds was killed and the battle was going adversely. We halted for the night about two miles from Gettysburg, and during the latter part of the march the sound of cannonading had been heard until nightfall.

At daylight next morning the command was moved into line of battle on the left of Cemetery Hill, overlooking the town of Gettysburg, and a line of skirmishers was deployed. The regiment was on the skirmish-line all day, but in the evening it was placed in position behind a low stone wall at the edge of an apple-orchard, and about three hundred yards west of General Meade's headquarters. The line fronted northwest, and faced the Emmittsburg road. In the afternoon our skirmishers were driven in by a strong line of the enemy, and while retiring, Captain Martin W. B. Ellegood, of Company E, fell mortally wounded. A sanguinary struggle then ensued in the peach-orchard on our left, which resulted in our favor, and at night a vigorous attack was made by the enemy upon the Twelfth Corps, posted on Culp's Hill, at our right.

On the morning of the 3d a dropping fire of skirmishers began at daylight, and continued, with an occasional shot from a battery, until ten o'clock, when all firing ceased, and an ominous quiet fell upon both armies. This silence was suddenly broken at half-past one o'clock by the report of a gun from the neighborhood of the seminary building, followed immediately by a simultaneous discharge from many batteries planted north, east, and west of our position. This fearful cannonade, and the charge that followed it, is called, and will always be known in history as the "high-water mark of the Rebellion." For three hours the enemy kept up an incessant fire of shot and shell on the centre, held by the Second Army Corps. About half-past four o'clock the fire of the batteries ceased, and the enemy's infantry marched across the plain and charged our line. We were cautioned to hold our fire until the rebels began to climb the fence along the Emmittsburg road. When this obstacle was reached their ranks were thrown into some confusion, when, at the word "Fire!" shouted by General Hays, commanding the division, such an appalling sheet of flame burst from our line that the rebel ranks melted away like wax, and none of them reached a point in our front nearer than fifty yards, though they succeeded in penetrating the line a few hundred yards on our left, near Little Round Top. The dreadful execution in our front was owing to the fact that the men of the First Delaware, Fourteenth Connecticut, and Twelfth New Jersey had collected all the spare guns, had prepared a large supply of cartridges, and laid them in rows beside them, and the men in the rear rank loaded the muskets as fast as those in front could fire them, and to the further fact that the Twelfth New Jersey Regiment was armed with smooth-bore Springfields, carrying buck and ball.

During this charge Colonel Smyth, commanding the brigade, was slightly wounded in the face by a piece of shell while restoring order in the ranks of a New York regiment which had given way on the right of their line. He went to the hospital after the firing had ceased, to have his wound dressed, and Lieutenant-Colonel F. E. Pierce, One Hundred and Eighth New York Volunteers, took command, and was in turn relieved by Colonel Dwight Morris, of the Fourteenth Connecticut Volunteers.

When the regiment entered the engagement at Gettysburg, it was commanded by Lieutenant-Colonel Harris; but before the battle ended it was commanded by a first lieutenant. Colonel Smyth was commanding the brigade, the lieutenant-colonel was placed in arrest for withdrawing from the skirmish-line with part of the regiment, Major Woodall was absent, wounded, and all the captains were absent, sick or wounded. Captain Hizar was wounded, and Captain Ellegood was killed, in the skirmish on the second day. First Lieutenant William Smith, of Company A, was in command of the regiment when he was killed by a cannon-shot during the charge on the 3d while carrying to brigade headquarters a rebel flag he had taken. This flag was stolen by a man of another regiment from the dead body of Lieutenant Smith after he fell, and was not included in the number of colors reported as cap-

tured by the regiment. The command then devolved
upon Lieutenant John T. Dent, of Company G.

When the rebel charge was broken and their ranks fell
into disorder, the First Delaware sprang over the stone
wall *en masse* and charged with the bayonet upon the rebel
fugitives, headed by Color-Sergeant John M. Dunn with
the national flag. A hand-to-hand conflict ensued, in which
numberless instances of gallantry occurred, and hundreds
of prisoners were sent to the rear.

It is simply impossible to conceive of a degree of bravery
or efficiency on the part of soldiers more exalted than that
shown by the entire brigade in meeting and overthrowing
this most desperate assault of the enemy, who manifested a
courage and skill no less admirable. Not a straggler nor a
skulker could be seen; every man was in the ranks, and,
when the masses of the enemy had crossed the fence on
the Emmittsburg road, although ordered to crouch close
behind the low stone wall, most of the men stood up-
right, as unsheltered as the enemy, and fired with regularity
and deadly precision.

The enemy's skirmishers occupied a house and barn near
the skirmish-line, about four hundred yards in front of our
position, and on the second day, the fire from these buildings becoming quite annoying, General Hays directed
Colonel Smyth to send a force and drive them out, which
was done, and nearly a hundred rebels captured; but later
in the day the enemy returned, announcing the fact by a
destructive fusilade from their shelter. General Hays
then ordered that the buildings should be retaken and
held, and for this duty the First Delaware and four com-

panies of the Twelfth New Jersey Volunteers were selected. Under a steady fire of sharpshooters they charged on the run, and captured another detachment of the enemy. The four companies of the Twelfth New Jersey Volunteers, under the command of Captain Richard Thompson, were left to hold the house, but were forced to retire on the approach of a strong body of the enemy, who again took possession of the stronghold. The Fourteenth Connecticut Volunteers was now ordered to dislodge the enemy and keep them out, which service they bravely executed.

While this detachment was charging on the buildings, and the fire from the enemy's line was exceedingly hot, General Hays called for a volunteer to carry an order to the commanding officer to burn the house and out-buildings. Captain J. Parke Postles, of the First Delaware, acting assistant inspector-general of the brigade, sprang on his horse, saying, "I will go, general!" and, bending forward, he rode in the face of that storm of lead, delivered the order, and, to the astonishment of all, returned unhurt.

There was little firing on the morning of the 4th, and plain indications were observed that the enemy was retreating. Our cavalry went in pursuit of them, while we spent the day in making field reports and inspections, burying the dead, bringing in the wounded, and collecting prisoners and arms.

The following is the report of Colonel Smyth of the part taken in the battle by the brigade:

HEADQUARTERS SECOND BRIGADE, THIRD DIVISION, SECOND ARMY CORPS,
July 17, 1863.
CAPTAIN G. P. CORTS, A.A.G.

CAPTAIN,—I have the honor to make the following report of the part taken in the action at Gettysburg, Pa., by this brigade from the 1st to the 4th of July, 1863.

Being in camp at Uniontown, Md., on the morning of July 1, 1863, I received an order to march at 6.30 A.M. Marched to Taneytown and halted until 12 M., when the command resumed the march towards Gettysburg, and encamped about three miles from the town. At 4 A.M. on the 2d the brigade was placed in position on the hill overlooking the town, my command being placed on the left of the First Brigade. This position we occupied until the termination of the action on the night of the 3d. Skirmishing commenced briskly along our front at 8 A.M. The First Delaware Volunteers was sent out as skirmishers, and the One Hundred and Eighth New York Volunteers was assigned to the support of Woodruff's Battery. At 2 P.M. the enemy opened upon us with a severe fire of artillery, accompanied by an advance of infantry, which drove in our skirmishers. They were, however, immediately replaced, and the enemy's skirmishers retired to their original position, except that a force of them retained possession of a large barn about four hundred yards in front of our line. Four companies of the Twelfth New Jersey Volunteers were sent to retake the barn and to dislodge the enemy's sharpshooters, which they succeeded in doing, capturing ninety-two prisoners, including seven commissioned officers. The enemy advanced, in turn, and reoccupied the barn. The First Delaware Volunteers and four more companies of the Twelfth New Jersey Volunteers, under the command of Captain Thompson, Twelfth New Jersey, were subsequently sent to again take possession of the barn, which they did, having taken ten prisoners, one of whom was a major. Observing that the enemy was moving in force along a ravine towards the barn, Captain Thompson thought proper to retire. Firing ceased about 9 P.M., the remainder of the night being quiet. Artillery-firing from both sides began at 4 A.M. on the morning of the 3d, the heaviest firing being on our right. Skirmishing with artillery and infantry continued all along the line until 10.30 A.M., when a lull ensued which lasted up to 2 P.M. The barn and house near it being reoccupied by the enemy's sharpshooters, an order was received from General Hays, commanding the division, to take the house and barn at all hazards, and hold it. The Fourteenth Connecticut Volunteers was detailed on this service, which it gallantly performed. Soon after an order came from General Hays to burn the house and barn, and they were accordingly fired. At 2 P.M. a most terrific cannonading was opened upon our front by the simultaneous discharge of a whole battery. This fire from an extended line of the enemy's batteries concentrated on the small space occupied by our troops, and continued without intermission until nearly 5 P.M. The officers and men behaved with the greatest coolness, and endured this terrible fire with much fortitude. As the fire from the enemy's batteries slackened their infantry moved upon our position, their line preceded by skirmishers. My men were directed to reserve their fire until the foe was within fifty yards, when, so effective and incessant was the fire delivered from my line, that the advancing enemy was staggered, thrown into confusion, and finally fled from the field, throwing away their arms in their flight. Many threw themselves on the ground to escape our destructive fire, and raised their hands in token of surrender. The number of prisoners captured by this brigade is estimated at from twelve to fifteen hundred, and the number of small-arms collected by them is estimated at two thousand. This command captured nine battle-flags, as follows, viz.: the Fourteenth Connecticut Volunteers, four; First Delaware Volunteers, three; and the Twelfth New Jersey Volunteers, two. The One Hundred and Eighth New York Volunteers rendered very efficient service while supporting Woodruff's Battery, and lost heavily, the casualties being one-half of the regiment in action. The men assisted in manœuvring the guns when so many of the horses were killed that the guns, limbers, and caissons could with difficulty be moved.

During the cannonading, having received a wound, I was obliged to quit the field, and surrendered the command to Lieutenant-Colonel F. E. Pierce, One Hundred and Eighth New York Volunteers.

The casualties in my command were as follows, viz.: On the brigade staff, two commissioned officers wounded. First Regiment, Delaware Volunteers, two commissioned officers killed, two wounded, and one missing; seven enlisted men killed, forty-one wounded, and ten missing. One Hundred and Eighth New York Volunteers, three commissioned officers killed and ten wounded, and thirteen enlisted men killed and seventy-six wounded. Fourteenth Connecticut Volunteers, ten commissioned officers wounded, and ten enlisted men killed, forty-two wounded, and four missing. Twelfth New

Jersey Volunteers, two commissioned officers killed, four wounded, and twenty-one enlisted men killed, seventy-five wounded, and eleven missing. Battalion, Tenth New York Volunteers, two enlisted men killed and four wounded. Total, seven officers killed, twenty-eight wounded, and one missing; fifty-three enlisted men killed, two hundred and thirty-eight wounded, and twenty-five missing. Aggregate, three hundred and fifty-two.

I desire to call the attention of the general commanding to the bravery, self-possession, and energy of Lieutenant-Colonel Francis E. Pierce, commanding the One Hundred and Eighth New York Volunteers, who throughout the heaviest of the fire showed the greatest unconcern, passing along his line and encouraging his men. Major John T. Hill, commanding the Twelfth New Jersey Volunteers, who directed his men to retain their fire during the charge of the enemy until they were within twenty yards, when at his command so tremendous a fire of buck and ball was poured into their ranks as to render it impossible that one of them could reach the breastwork. Major Theodore G. Ellis, commanding the Fourteenth Connecticut Volunteers, who led the last attack on the house and barn occupied by the enemy's sharpshooters in a very spirited manner, completely routing them. Lieutenant William Smith, who commanded the First Delaware Volunteers during the attack upon our front. He was a brave and efficient officer, and was instantly killed, with one of the enemy's captured flags in his hand.

I would also particularly mention the able and efficient services of the gentlemen composing my staff: Lieutenant William P. Seville, Acting Assistant Adjutant-General; Captain James Parke Postles, Acting Assistant Inspector-General; Lieutenant Charles S. Schaeffer, Aide-de-Camp, who was wounded; and Lieutenant Theron E. Parsons, Aide-de-Camp. These officers are deserving of much credit for their conduct during the whole action. Lieutenant W. P. Seville and Captain J. P. Postles I wish especially to recommend to your notice as really meritorious officers.

I am, sir, very respectfully,

Your obedient servant,

THOMAS A. SMYTH,

Colonel First Delaware Volunteers, Commanding Brigade.

Owing to the fact that the officers in command of the regiment at Gettysburg were so frequently changed by the casualties of the action, no official report from the regiment was made before its discharge from the service; but when Colonel Batchelder was appointed by the War Department to prepare an official history of this celebrated battle, he called on Lieutenant (then Major) Dent for a report, and the following was submitted, viz.:

————, 1863.

SIR,—I have the honor to submit the following as the report of the part taken by the First Regiment, Delaware Infantry, at the battle of Gettysburg:

On the evening of July 1st the regiment, under command of Lieutenant-Colonel E. P. Harris, bivouacked to the right of the Taneytown road, within three miles of Gettysburg.

Early on the morning of July 2d the line of march was resumed. We arrived on the field about 4 A.M., when we were massed in column behind Woodruff's Battery, in which position we lay for about an hour. We then moved a short distance to the left, when we were deployed as skirmishers, some five hundred yards in front of the main line, where we remained actively engaged during the entire day.

About 4 P.M., the ammunition of the men being exhausted, Lieutenant-Colonel Harris withdrew the right wing of the regiment from the skirmish-line, for which he was placed under arrest by General Hancock. The command then devolved on Captain Thomas B. Hizar, of Company I. We were then assigned position in the line of battle behind a fallen stone wall, to the left of Woodruff's and right of Arnold's batteries. About dark the left wing of the regiment was driven in off the skirmish-line. Captain Hizar, commanding the regiment, was about this time wounded. He remained in command until 11 P.M., when he retired. The command then devolved on Lieutenant William Smith, Company A.

During the day the regiment lost in commissioned officers one killed (Captain M. W. B. Ellegood), three wounded, and one taken prisoner; four enlisted men killed, thirteen wounded, and ten prisoners.

During the night of the 2d and the day of the 3d the regiment remained in the same position, and it was there it received the united attack of Pickett's and Pender's columns. These columns overlapped in our immediate front, and made the pressure on our line very heavy, the Pickett column moving on us in an oblique direction from the left, the Pender column moving on us in an oblique direction from the right, both columns converging in our immediate front.

The regiment, however, with iron will, stubbornly maintained its position and repulsed the combined attack. As soon as the charge of the enemy was broken the regiment sprang over the wall and gave them a countercharge, capturing many prisoners and five battle-flags. It was in this charge that Lieutenant William Smith, commanding the regiment, fell, and when picked up, his sword was found in one hand and a captured rebel flag in the other.

The command then devolved upon John T. Dent, the first lieutenant of Company G. Late in the afternoon of the third day the regiment was ordered to charge on the ruins of the burnt barn in our front, and dislodged a small body of the enemy who were occupying the same, and annoying our relief-parties engaged in bringing in and relieving the wounded. This object accomplished, the command returned to the main line, where they remained during the night.

On the morning of the 4th Lieutenant-Colonel Harris was restored to the command. Special mention should be made of Captain M. W. B. Ellegood, Company E, who fell on the skirmish-line, and Lieutenant William Smith, who commanded the regiment during the charge, and fell mortally wounded with a captured flag in his hand, and of First Lieutenant Andrew Wall, who, though not on duty, by his coolness and presence gave encouragement to the men. Also of Color-Sergeant John M. Dunn, who, colors in hand, led the regiment across the stone wall in its countercharge; and of Color-Sergeant Thomas Seymour, who was cut in two by a shell; and Privates William Williams, of Company A; B. McCarren, of Company C; and J. B. Mayberry, of Company F, who each captured flags.

During the two days' fight the regiment lost, commissioned officers, two killed, four wounded, and one taken prisoner; enlisted men, ten killed, forty-one wounded, and ten taken prisoners; total, twelve killed, forty-five wounded, and eleven prisoners.

The enemy's losses in our front were very severe. The ground was literally black with killed and wounded.

Your obedient servant,

JOHN T. DENT,

Late Major First Delaware Volunteer Infantry, and Lieutenant Company G, Commanding Regiment at battle of Gettysburg.

The official report of Colonel Smyth gives the number of enlisted men killed at Gettysburg as seven, but the muster-out rolls show ten killed, and that three others died of wounds shortly after the action, as follows: Corporal Adam Huhn and Private William Williams, of Company A; Sergeant Thomas Seymour and Private James Simpson, of Company B; Private James Dougherty, of Company C; Privates William D. Dorsey and John Shulty, of Company D; Private Thomas P. Carey, of Company E; Corporal John Stein, of Company H; and Private John S. Black, of Company K. Those who died afterwards from the effects of wounds were Sergeants Benjamin B. Sempler and David M. Sempler, of Company E, and Sergeant Wellington G. Lloyd, of Company G.

THE PURSUIT TO THE RAPPAHANNOCK.

Our corps did not start in pursuit of the flying foe until four o'clock on the 5th, and then it marched but a short distance, to Two Taverns, where it encamped. Learning that the heavy rains that followed the battle had so swollen the Potomac that the rebel pontoon bridge had been swept away and that the river was too high to ford, the ardor of the pursuit was abated in some degree; at all events, the Second Corps remained in camp all day on the 6th. The command marched at 5 A.M. on the 7th, and halted at Taneytown for a fresh supply of rations. Next day the route was again taken, and in that and the two days following we passed through Frederick, Bruceville, Jefferson, Burketsville, Rohrersville, and Keedysville, and encamped about three miles from the field of Antietam, where,

as an attack from the enemy was apprehended, we took up
a defensive position.   On the 11th our route lay through
Tilghmanton to Jones' Creek, where we again made preparations to receive an attack.   During the afternoon heavy
skirmishing occurred on our left, and after dark the command moved a mile farther to the front, and took position
in line of battle at two o'clock on the morning of the 12th.
Then followed what seemed to be undecided movements,
marching to and fro in the drenching rain until night, when
we began vigorously to work at throwing up intrenchments, at which labor the entire night was spent, only to
abandon them in the morning and move nearer to the
enemy's lines, where our brigade was held in reserve
throughout the 13th.

About ten o'clock at night an order was received directing
a general charge on the rebel works at daylight in the
morning, in which no other weapon was to be used than
the bayonet; the men being required to take out of their
cartridge-boxes all the ammunition and turn it in.   This
order was countermanded just before daylight, in all re-
spects excepting that in regard to marching.   The troops
moved forward in line of battle, passed through the deserted
earth-works of the confederates and continued to Falling
Waters, where we went into camp, possessed of the unques-
tionable fact that the rebel army had just completed a
successful crossing of the river, with the comparatively
trifling loss of about two thousand prisoners.

The army marched early on the morning of the 15th,
passed through Downsville, Fairplay, Bakersville, Sharpsburg, Harper's Ferry, Sandy Hook, and encamped near

Maryland Heights, where the 17th was spent in drawing supplies and making out returns and muster-rolls. The Potomac was again crossed on the 18th, and the column halted for the night at Hillsboro'. Thus the army followed Lee, passing through Woodbury, Bloomfield, Upperville, Ashby's Gap, and reaching Manassas Gap on the 23d.

While marching up and down these mountain roads on the 23d and 24th, endeavoring to get a chance to catch the enemy in flank through one of the gaps, the suffering of the men can scarcely be depicted. During these two days the First Delaware marched altogether as skirmishers or flankers. The roads were rough and rocky, the streams to be forded were numerous, much of the ground passed over was wet and boggy, the rations were exhausted, and everybody was out of humor and hungry. At this time an order was published cautioning the troops to economize their rations, which produced no little grumbling and profanity, since they had no rations to be economical with. In the evening a facetious member of the First came to the colonel and asked permission for himself and five comrades to make a short circuit in the neighborhood for the purpose of economizing their rations.

The line of march was continued through Springfield, Rectortown, White Plains, and the column arrived at Warrenton Junction on the 26th, where a halt of several days was made to issue rations and send details north for conscripts.

On the 27th of July an order was received to consolidate the regiment into a battalion of five companies, and to muster out the colonel, major, five captains, and ten lieutenants, together with all surplus non-commissioned officers and musicians ; but when it was shown to the commander-in-chief by the division and corps commanders what injustice this would be to several excellent and valuable officers, and that they would rather have the regiment filled up than reduced, the order was temporarily countermanded.   At this time Colonel Smyth was recommended very warmly for promotion to the rank of brigadier-general of volunteers, and Adjutant Seville for appointment as captain and assistant adjutant-general.   Major Woodall was assigned to command the Thirty-ninth New York Volunteers (which was attached to the Third Brigade) on the 30th of July, but returned to the regiment a few weeks afterwards.

August 1st the division marched through Morrisville to Elktown, and the Third Brigade kept on to Bristersburg, and there encamped, furnishing a picket-line from that town to Cedar Run.   It became evident that a prolonged stay was intended at this place, for orders were given to permit the troops to make themselves as comfortable as possible, and a detail of three officers and six men was sent to Smyrna, Del., for drafted men to fill the depleted ranks of the regiment.   The brigade remained in camp here until September 12th, when marching orders were received, and the command proceeded through Rappahannock Station, Culpeper Court-House, and on to Cedar Mountain ; and on the 18th, to the Rapidan River, where once more our picket-line confronted that of the enemy posted on the other side. Here the brigade was encamped, keeping watch of the enemy until the 4th of October.   But few changes had taken place among the officers of the regiment since July.

Second Lieutenant George T. Price, of Company A, was advanced to first lieutenant on July 3d; on the 18th of July First Lieutenant Andrew Walls was discharged, and on the 31st, Captain Allen Shortledge, of Company G, was transferred to the Invalid Corps, and First Lieutenant John T. Dent was promoted to captain. Second Lieutenant Benjamin Y. Draper, of Company D, was transferred to Company H, as first lieutenant, August 8th, and September 13th, First Lieutenant Charles B. Tanner resigned. On the 21st, Adjutant William P. Seville was promoted to captain of Company E, and First Lieutenant Charles S. Schaeffer, of Company I, was appointed adjutant. Second Lieutenant John Hart, of Company F, was dismissed on the 22d, Second Lieutenant James D. Simpson, of Company D, was advanced to first lieutenant on the 23d, and Sergeant Matthew W. Macklem, of Company B, was promoted to second lieutenant, and again, on the 28th, to first lieutenant.

The brigade broke camp at 7 A.M. on the 4th of October, and marched beyond Culpeper, and on the 10th orders for marching were received, accompanied by signs of either an extended march or a battle. It was soon known that the rebels had set out again, bent on northern invasion, and were endeavoring to gain as much distance in advance of us as they had in June; but on this occasion they failed, for their advance had not taken the route more than six hours before our army was in pursuit, and the entire movement became a foot-race for possession of the strong battle heights along Bull Run, and, as usual, the Second Corps had the post of honor as rear-guard of the army.

The command started on the 10th, and marched but a

few miles, and next day it crossed the Rappahannock and pressed forward to Bealton Station. On the 12th we suddenly turned backward and recrossed the river, where we stood in order of battle all day, as the rebels had appeared on our rear in strong force, and had fought a desperate battle with General Kilpatrick's cavalry. At midnight, instead of the sleep and rest we so much needed, we marched again, once more crossing the Rappahannock, moving northward, and skirmished with the enemy until dark.

THE BATTLE OF BRISTOE STATION.

The column moved at the break of dawn, and immediately ran against the enemy at Auburn, where we had a sharp skirmish for about two hours, when the rebels concluded to take another road. The march was resumed, but did not continue long, for at Bristoe Station the column was attacked on the left flank by the enemy, who was posted in force on a hill overlooking the railroad. The column formed line of battle, facing the left, and took possession of the railroad embankment. Our brigade advanced through a thick wood toward the enemy's position, and was directed to halt in the wood until the line in an open field on our left could connect with us. While waiting here for the word to advance, Captain William F. Smith, of Company C, and Lieutenant-Colonel Thomas H. Davis, of the Twelfth New Jersey, asked and received permission to take parts of the two regiments and charge upon a battery the enemy had posted on the hill to the right near the edge of the wood. They made the attack in fine style, simultaneously with a force from the First Division, and captured the battery. This detachment joined the command just in time to move forward. The action soon grew quite hot with musketry-fire, but the enemy steadily and slowly fell back, and finally retreated in haste and confusion, and our forces took possession of their camp-ground, and captured one hundred and fifty prisoners of Hill's corps.

The following is Colonel Smyth's report of this action:

HEADQUARTERS SECOND BRIGADE, THIRD DIVISION, SECOND A. C.,
October 17, 1863.

CAPTAIN GEORGE P. CORTS,
    ASSISTANT ADJUTANT-GENERAL THIRD DIVISION.

CAPTAIN,—I have the honor to make the following report of the part taken by this brigade in the actions of the 14th of October, at Turkey Creek and Bristoe Station:

The command marched from camp on the Warrenton road at daylight on the morning of the 14th of October. While crossing Turkey Creek the enemy opened on the column with artillery. An order was received from Brigadier-General Hays, commanding the division, to deploy skirmishers on the right and left flanks of the column. I accordingly deployed five companies of the First Delaware Volunteers, under the command of Major Woodall, and the One Hundred and Eighth New York Volunteers, under the command of Colonel Powers,—the First Delaware on the left and the One Hundred and Eighth New York on the right. The Fourteenth Connecticut Volunteers was formed in line of battle with the right resting on the road; and, as the enemy commenced a fire of musketry farther to the left, the First Delaware skirmishers were extended by the left flank, and the Twelfth New Jersey Volunteers was formed in line of battle facing to the left, with the right resting on the left of the Fourteenth Connecticut. Receiving an order from General Hays to send a regiment to the support of the One Hundred and Twenty-sixth New York Volunteers, I sent the Twelfth New Jersey Volunteers for this service. The order was then given by General Hays to advance by a flank on the road, and throw flankers out on the right. The skirmishers of the First Delaware were withdrawn from the left and deployed as flankers on the right. The column then moved on.

About 3 P.M., as the command was marching by a flank from a wood toward the railroad, near Bristoe Station, the enemy suddenly attacked the column with artillery. General Hays ordered me to form line of battle to the left and advance. As the brigade debouched from the wood I marched it by the left flank. Owing to the right of the brigade marching in line of battle while the left was obliged to move forward into line as it came out of the wood, some little disorder was occasioned, which was, however, soon rectified, and the brigade was formed into line along the railroad. A column of the enemy appeared on a hill in our front and a little to our right, and opened a fire of musketry. An order was received from General Hays to move forward through the wood and charge that column of the enemy on their right flank. I ordered my command to fix bayonets and advance through the wood. The line was formed in the wood, the First Delaware on the right, and the following regiments in succession to the left: Fourteenth Connecticut, Twelfth New Jersey, and One Hundred and Eighth New York. A regiment of the Second Division, the Seventh Michigan, came to the front at this point. They had been deployed as flankers. As there was an interval between the Twelfth New Jersey and One Hundred and Eighth New York, I placed the Seventh Michigan there to complete the connection, thinking that more service could be obtained by forming it in the line here than by permitting it, in the emergency, to fall back to seek its brigade. This regiment was commanded by Major S. W. Curtis, who seemed anxious to perform his share in the action wherever circumstances might place him. His regiment fought well. Colonel C. J. Powers, One Hundred and Eighth New York Volunteers, reported a force of the enemy moving toward our left, and several musket-shots were fired into the One Hundred and Eighth New York, wounding one or two men. I reported this to General Hays, who directed me to make such disposition as would meet the enemy. I then ordered the One Hundred and Eighth New York, Seventh Michigan, and two companies of the Twelfth New Jersey to file to the left. Finding that skirmishers from the First Division were deployed in our front, I cautioned the command against firing unless they were sure they saw the enemy. About this time the skirmishers of the Third Brigade were advancing to capture one of the enemy's batteries, and in order to prevent the enemy in our front from moving

7

to the rescue of the battery, my line was advanced to the open space on the side of the wood toward the enemy. A rebel line then made its appearance about four hundred yards from my line, their line of battle running diagonally to mine, their right being closer to us than their left, at which my command opened a severe fire of musketry upon them, and arrested their progress. Receiving an order from General Hays to halt my command and hold the position, I did so. Soon afterwards I received an order from General Hays to fall back and take position along the railroad. This was accordingly executed, the brigade retiring to its new position in good order. About dark the enemy opened upon us with a battery, which did but little injury, however, before it was silenced.

About 8 P.M. an order was received to prepare to resume the march, following the Third Brigade. At 10.30 the march commenced quietly and in perfect order, and the command continued to Bull Run, where it bivouacked at 3 A.M. on the morning of the 15th.

One hundred and thirty-five men of different regiments of the Second Division, Third Corps, who had straggled from their commands, were assembled at Turkey Creek, and assigned temporarily to this brigade. I attached them to the Twelfth New Jersey Volunteers, and they were joined to several companies. Many of these men again dropped out from the regiment when going into action, but the majority of them remained and fought bravely. Of these, one man was killed and three wounded, but, owing to the activity of the day, no opportunity offered to get their names, company, or regiment.

In concluding my report I deem it but justice to mention to the general commanding the division the efficient services and gallant conduct of Colonel Charles J. Powers, commanding the One Hundred and Eighth New York, Lieutenant-Colonel Thomas H. Davis, commanding the Twelfth New Jersey, Colonel Theodore G. Ellis, commanding the Fourteenth Connecticut Volunteers, and Major Daniel Woodall, of the First Delaware. Each of these officers are entitled to much credit for the promptness with which they executed my orders, and the energy and zeal with which they labored to secure success.

Considering the suddenness of the attack, the difficulties under which the command was formed, the density of the wood through which it moved, and remembering that a large portion of it were untried soldiers, I think the troops behaved very well indeed.

I would also respectfully recommend to your notice the gentlemen of my staff, Captain William P. Seville, A.A.A.G., Captain John L. Sparks, A.A.I.G., Lieutenant Theron E. Parsons, A.D.C., and Lieutenant Edward M. Dubois, A.D.C. Their conduct was cool and self-possessed and their services meritorious.

I have the honor to forward herewith a nominal list of the killed, wounded, and missing of my brigade.

I am, captain, very respectfully,

Your obedient servant,

THOMAS A. SMYTH,

Colonel First Delaware Volunteers, Commanding Brigade.

The only member of the regiment killed in this action was Corporal William Darlington, of Company F.

About 9 P.M. the command again took the road in a steady rain, and marched rapidly, notwithstanding the depth and tenacity of the mud, reaching the hills on Bull Run before daylight. Fortunately, the Army of the Potomac had out-marched Lee's veterans and won the race. Our lines were advantageously posted in the vicinity of the old battle-grounds, and after two or three spirited attacks on the 15th, and several efforts to out-manœuvre us on the 16th, 17th, and 18th, the rebels became discouraged and commenced their retreat on the 19th, followed closely by the Federal army, the Second Corps in advance, and our brigade, throughout the whole day's march, nearly a mile in advance of the corps.

OPERATIONS ON MINE RUN AND RE-ENLISTMENT.

The brigade arrived at Warrenton on the 23d of October, and laid out a formal camp, everything indicating that a prolonged stay was intended at this place, and these indications were verified by the army lying at rest for two weeks. Marching orders overtook us, however, on the 6th of November, and next morning the command set out, our brigade again leading the corps. The enemy was found at Kelly's Ford on the Rappahannock, and a brisk engagement occurred, in which the rebels seem to have been taken by surprise, for they were speedily routed and about four hundred prisoners of North Carolina troops were captured. The river was crossed on the 8th, and the line of march pursued to Mountain Creek, where the corps went into camp on the 10th, and continued there until the 26th. On that day the command once more started southward, crossed the Rapidan River at Germania Ford, and encountered the enemy next day at Robinson's Tavern, where we formed line of battle; the First Delaware were thrown forward as skirmishers, and were constantly engaged with the enemy's line until night. Before morning the rebels had fallen back, and we started in hot pursuit, the First Delaware again in advance as skirmishers. This was an extremely fatiguing march to our regiment, passing for several miles in an extended line of battle, over all kinds of obstacles, always on the very heels of the retreating foe, and when, at length, the rebel position was reached late in the afternoon, the men were relieved from their exhausting and perilous duty by the One Hundred and Eighth New York Volunteers. But little time was allowed them for rest; before daylight on the 29th the corps set out, making a wide detour through woods and valleys, until late in the afternoon we reached New Verdiersville, on the extreme right of the rebel line. It was intended that the Second Corps should reach the right and rear of the enemy on

Mine Run about noon and attack, in co-operation with the rest of the army, which was to charge in front ; but the muddy wood-roads over which the command had to pass so delayed our progress that our destination was not attained until it was too late to attack.   Orders were received that the works of the enemy should be stormed at half-past four o'clock next morning, and that no fires should be made.   This latter portion of the order was very severe on the men, as the night was so cold that ice was formed.

At early daylight line of battle was formed in silence at the edge of the narrow skirt of wood which separated us from the rebel line, and the troops were kept in line in readiness for the word to move forward.   Bayonets were fixed, knapsacks were unslung and stacked in piles by companies.   Nearly every man of the First Delaware had a piece of paper pinned on his breast, containing his name, company, and regiment, in order that his body might be known in case of his death.   This precaution was adopted without orders by the men themselves, who well knew the unusually perilous nature of the charge then about to be made.   There was much delay about making this assault. The enemy had discovered our presence early the previous night, and had been working with desperate energy all night long, building breastworks and slashing the timber to construct abatis.   At daylight their works were reconnoitred, and found to be too strong to attack with any hope of success.   Finally the charge was abandoned, and the troops withdrawn to the ground which they occupied the preceding night.   During the day the rebels made a movement looking to an attack on the rear of our position, whereupon the First Delaware was deployed in the rear as skirmishers.

On the evening of the 2d of December the command received orders to march at once, leaving the camp-fires burning, and the First Delaware Regiment to hold the skirmish-line, and follow the column about midnight, acting as rear-guard. Colonel Smyth remained with the regiment and took charge of withdrawing the skirmish-line in the darkness, and in the face of a wary and watchful foe, which duty was successfully accomplished, the regiment overtaking the brigade just before sunrise.

Corporal Evan P. Grubb, of Company H, behaved in a very gallant manner in the dangerous duty of maintaining and withdrawing at the proper time the strong picket-line, after the troops had silently departed from the enemy's front, and was warmly commended by Colonel Smyth.

The army returned to its former camp near Mountain Creek, and on the 4th it took up a line of occupation, which changed the position of our brigade to Stevensburg, where we settled down into winter quarters, and a city of huts and adobe houses sprang into existence within the next fortnight.

December 18th two hundred and ten officers and men of the regiment were discharged, and remustered as veterans for three years or during the war. Some weeks previously, before the Mine Run campaign, the government had published to the army an offer to grant all veterans whose term of service had not expired a bounty of three hundred dollars and thirty days' leave of absence if they would volunteer for another term of three years. The First Delaware

Regiment was the first organization in the Army of the Potomac to embrace this offer, and on the 29th of December that part of the regiment which had re-enlisted started home, with instructions to report to the Governor of Delaware. Those of the regiment who declined to re-enlist marched on the same day with the brigade to Stony Mountain, where it occupied an isolated position, charged with the duty of guarding Morton's Ford.

The regiment arrived in Wilmington, January 1, 1864, and was most enthusiastically received by the warm-hearted and patriotic citizens; marched through the city amid the firing of cannon, the ringing of bells, and through streets densely thronged, to the town-hall, where an elegant and bountiful dinner was spread for them. A splendid set of colors was presented to the regiment on this occasion, which, after passing through the storms of many fierce and bloody battles, was brought back with the survivors of the regiment, bearing the stains and rents of the terrible struggles through which it had passed, and is now consigned to the care of the State Historical Society, in whose custody it will rest in peace until crumbled to dust by the destroying hand of time.

At the close of the public dinner and reception the arms and equipments were stored away, and the command was dismissed for the remainder of the month's furlough.

Captain William Y. Swiggett, of Company F, was transferred to the Veteran Reserve Corps October 12, 1863, and on the 28th Lieutenant-Colonel Edward P. Harris resigned on account of disability. On November 6th Major Daniel Woodall was promoted to lieutenant-colonel; Captain William F. Smith, of Company C, was promoted to major; First Lieutenant George T. Price, of Company A, was made captain of Company C; First Lieutenant Matthew W. Macklem, of Company B, was raised to captain of Company F; and Quartermaster-Sergeant Washington F. Williamson was made first lieutenant of Company A. On November 20th First Lieutenant James Lewis, of Company C, was transferred to the Veteran Reserve Corps.

At the expiration of the veteran furlough the officers and men reported to Colonel Smyth, at Wilmington, for duty from a week before the time fixed upon for returning to the front up to the very moment of taking the cars, and few failed to return, as several of the absentees joined the regiment after it had reached the army. The regiment went into camp on the 5th of February, and on the 9th started on its return to the field, where it arrived on the 12th, and found the brigade encamped on Stony Mountain. Our return to camp was the occasion of quite a jubilee of welcome, discipline being considerably relaxed to permit a free expression of the pleasure old comrades felt in the reunion. Not all the members of the regiment that we parted from in December were there to greet us, for there had been a sharp action with the enemy, brought on by a reconnoissance in force at Morton's Ford, February 6th, and several men of the regiment had been wounded and were sent away to hospitals.

The Second Army Corps gave a ball at Brandy Plains on the evening of the 22d, which was a grand affair, and was attended by many civil dignitaries from Washington, accompanied by their ladies, and on the following day a grand review of the corps was held, in honor of our distinguished visitors.

With the approach of spring a perceptible increase in activity was observable among the staff departments, and the signs of the time denoted an early opening of the campaign. Portions of the army were in motion as early as the 28th, and our brigade was ordered to be in readiness for moving with three days' cooked rations.

March 26th the First and Second Brigades were consolidated; Colonel Smyth was assigned to the command of the Irish Brigade, and our brigade received for its commander Colonel Samuel S. Carroll, of the Eighth Ohio Volunteers, formerly of the regular army, a brave, genial, and able officer, and the following regiments were henceforth associated with us: Eighth Ohio, Fourth Ohio, Twentieth Massachusetts, Seventh West Virginia, and Fourteenth Indiana. April 14th the brigade was reviewed by Brigadier-General Gibbon. General Hancock reviewed the division next day, and on the 22d the corps passed in review before General Grant.

THE WILDERNESS AND SPOTTSYLVANIA.

At midnight on May 3d the first movement in the grand campaign began. Our brigade marched to join the division, and the column continued on its route to Ely's Ford, where we crossed the Rapidan and bivouacked at night on the battle-field of Chancellorsville.

Next morning the troops were in motion at half-past four, the Second Corps marching to Todd's Tavern, where line of battle was formed to support the cavalry, but about noon orders were received to march with all speed back to the Plank Road, and report to General D. B. Birney. On arriving by the Brock Road, the brigade was ordered to advance on the right of the Plank Road, the left of our line on the road. The brigade advanced in the following order, running from left to right: first line, Tenth New York and Twelfth New Jersey; second line, Fourteenth Connecticut, First Delaware, and One Hundred and Eighth New York; third line, Seventh West Virginia, Fourteenth Indiana, and Eighth Ohio. The Nineteenth Maine Volunteers, a very large regiment, was ordered to report to Colonel Carroll, and was placed in the fourth line. Our lines had not moved more than fifty yards down a gentle slope towards a swamp, and through a dense thicket of scrub-oak and dwarf-pine, when the enemy, who were in position on the opposite edge of the swamp, opened upon us a terrific fire of musketry by volleys. This fire thinned our ranks very perceptibly; but we returned it with interest. No artillery or cavalry could be brought into action, owing to the closeness of the wood and thickness of the undergrowth; the only weapon used was the musket, but this was handled with deadly effect, because of the near proximity of the opposing lines. A continuous fire, varied at intervals with volleys, was kept up until sunset, when the fire from the enemy slackened. An immediate forward movement was ordered, the rebels retreating before us, and night overtook us, closing the action, and leaving us in possession of the field.

In this action Colonel Carroll was slightly wounded in the arm, but would not quit the field. That night we slept on our arms upon the ground we held when the battle ceased.

At half-past four o'clock on the morning of May 6th we formed our line for an advance, and pushed forward over the crest of the hill, the enemy retiring. On the rise of the next hill the line was moved by the left flank across the Plank Road. While making this change of position our left was suddenly charged by an overwhelming force of the enemy, and forced back upon the centre. Here the confusion was checked, and the rebels were held at bay by continuous and desperate exertions. Our ranks were growing thin and our ammunition was almost exhausted, when, a little past nine o'clock, we were relieved by the Ninth Corps, and directed to retire to the Brock Road and remain in reserve. The brigade halted about three hundred yards from the road, stacked arms, rested, refilled cartridge-boxes and canteens, made out casualty lists, and looked after the wounded.

About three o'clock in the afternoon the troops in the front gave way, Longstreet's corps having charged the temporary breastwork which had been thrown up along the Brock Road; they were held in check for some time, but they finally succeeded in breaking our line near and on the left of the Plank Road, and capturing two or three batteries. At this moment orders were received by Colonel Carroll to charge the enemy and retake our breastworks; the men hurried into line at the command "Fall in!" and when Colonel Carroll's stentorian voice rang out, "Forward, double-quick, charge!" the brigade swept down the hill like an avalanche. A few minutes' bloody work and the rebels were routed, pursued to the edge of the woods, and several of our guns recaptured. Thus ended the battle of the Wilderness.

The good conduct of Sergeant William Caywood, of Company A, during the engagement was generally remarked, and after his return to the regiment from absence on account of wounds received in this action, he was rewarded with well-merited promotion to a commission.

Lieutenant Charles J. Steel, of Company E, was conspicuous for bravery in the first day's struggle, and was mortally wounded. Though commissioned but a few weeks previously, he was a promising officer, and his loss was deeply felt.

The gallantry of First Lieutenant James Kettlewood, of Company C, won him the warm commendations of his superior officers; he, also, was badly wounded on the second day of the battle.

The loss of the brigade in the fighting of the 5th and 6th was seven hundred and twenty-seven, and in the First Delaware the following-named enlisted men were killed, or died subsequently of wounds then received: Killed, Sergeant John Webb, and Privates Jacob D. McKee and Robert Shaw, of Company A; Corporal Nicholas P. Howard, and Privates Enoch Chaffins and Martin Daily, of Company B; Sergeant John Carey, Company E; Corporal John Rhoads, Company F; Private Thomas Thornton, Company I; and Privates William C. Foreaker and George McColen, Company K. Died of wounds, Private Benjamin Cox, Company A; Private Joshua C. Aurtisto, Company D; Private William Weigle, Company G; Private Douglass White, Company H; and Private John Berwagner, Company I. Sixteen in all.

We set out at 6 A.M. of the 8th on the flanking movement, endeavoring to get upon the enemy's right and rear. Formed line of battle at Todd's Tavern, but shortly after noon received orders to make a forced march to Spottsylvania Court-House, where the Fifth Corps had grappled with Longstreet. We reached our destination at sunset and bivouacked for the night. Next day was spent in manœuvring for the advantage, in which our share was to march back to Todd's Tavern, then away to the right four or five miles, and at last, about four o'clock, to the Po River, where, in support of the First Division, we charged the enemy's rifle-pits, took them, and spent the night at Amity. During the afternoon our brigade was honored by the presence of Generals Grant, Meade, Hancock, and Gibbon.

From this time until the fall of Petersburg and Richmond some portions of the army were almost constantly engaged, and all were more or less under fire. On the 10th we stormed the enemy's works at Spottsylvania and were repulsed, though our line retained its position within fifty yards of the rebel intrenchments through the night, the picket-lines being so close that the men of the two armies held conversation, and sang their favorite songs for each other's entertainment.

Marching orders came on the evening of the 11th to move to the left with all possible silence, and a night march brought us at the early dawn to the Landrum House, where we quietly formed line behind a range of hills which concealed our movements from the enemy. The First

Division formed double column of battalions, and our division formed in line as support. In the gray dawn we advanced, taking the double-quick across a valley, and, with a tremendous cheer, charged the rebel works on the opposite crest; passed over their intrenchments, turning upon them their own guns, rushed directly into their camp and took them completely by surprise. Our captures included two brigadier-generals, Edward Johnson and G. H. Stewart, nearly all of an entire division, "Stonewall" Jackson's old brigade, sixteen flags, and eighteen cannons.

In this charge Sergeant David Riggs, of Company D, was color-sergeant, and just before the advance began he said, " I'll plant this on the rebel breastworks or die in the attempt." He was killed near the slope of the enemy's work, and another member of the color-guard carried the flag upon the crest.

A field-officer of one of the regiments in our (Third) brigade reported to brigade headquarters at the close of this action, that " the First Delaware captured a whole rebel regiment, colonel and all, with his sword and colors; that they had also captured a battery, but could not get the guns over the breastwork, so they cut all the horses loose, ran off all they could, and shot the rest."

Captain Matthew W. Macklem, of Company F, won much praise for his bravery and efficiency during the battles at Spottsylvania Court-House, where he received a severe wound.

On the 13th, while making a reconnoissance in force with the brigade, Colonel Carroll was badly wounded in his other arm, and was carried from the field. Before departing for the hospital, Colonel Carroll requested that Colonel Smyth be restored to the command of the brigade, and a promise was given him that his wishes should be complied with, which was done four days afterwards.   On the departure of Colonel Carroll, who was much esteemed and respected by his brigade, Colonel T. G. Ellis, of the Fourteenth Connecticut, was placed in command.

For a few days we were shifting position, at least once every day; on the 15th we were posted as a guard to the rear of the army; on the 16th we marched to the Second and Fifth Corps hospitals and brought away about six hundred wounded men.   Colonel Smyth resumed command of the brigade on the 17th, and Lieutenant Benjamin Y. Draper was appointed an aide-de-camp on his staff.

The command was aroused at 10 P.M. on the night of the 18th with orders to march.   The column started at midnight for the Landrum House and formed by battalions in mass, and at early daylight we deployed into line by battalions in mass to support the Corcoran Legion, which formed the first line to storm the works of the enemy.   Just before sunrise the charge was made, but the rebels were wary this time and on their guard, and the attack was repulsed with serious loss.   We lay under a fire of artillery and musketry until 12.35 P.M., when we withdrew beyond musket-range, reformed, and rested; but at 10 P.M. we started again, and made a night march to Anderson's Mills, about four miles to the left, where we took a position that indicated another charge.   The First Delaware was sent on picket duty, but the brigade did not march until 6 P.M., at which time we received sudden orders, and were hurried off to the right to look after Ewell's corps, which had attempted a flanking movement to our rear on the Fredericksburg pike. The Fourth Division of our corps had met Ewell, and showed such a determined spirit that the rebel commander changed his mind about marching any farther in that direction, leaving us free to return to our old camp.

FIGHTING OUR WAY TO PETERSBURG.

It was found that the enemy's works at Spottsylvania were too strong to allow of the possibility of bringing on an action that could be made decisive, so another flanking movement began at 11.20 A.M. on the 21st, and marching left in front, we passed Guiney's Station, Milford, through Bowling Green, crossed the river Ny, and intrenched. Next morning the First Delaware and One Hundred and Eighth New York Regiments were left to hold the line and complete the intrenchments, while the rest of the brigade pushed three miles to the front on a reconnoissance, returning to camp at night. The line of march was taken up at seven o'clock next morning, and the enemy was found posted in force in a strong position on the North Anna River. The artillery directed upon them an effective fire during the afternoon, and in the evening we made a demonstration on the bridge, at which the rebels set it afire and it was consumed from shore to shore.

At 7 A.M., May 24th, orders were received to construct a bridge, which was soon completed; the Eighth Ohio Volunteers crossed, deployed as skirmishers, and took possession of the enemy's earth-works with little opposition. The brigade then passed over and another advance was made to find the enemy.   They were encountered about a mile from the shore, and an engagement commenced which lasted until dark.   During this contest regiment after regiment was sent to Colonel Smyth from other brigades, so that by nightfall Colonel Smyth was in command of an entire division.   The action closed with the field in our possession, and during the night our lines were much strengthened. In the morning another forward movement was made in force, and the rebels were pushed over a mile farther, but at dark the whole command returned across the North Anna River.

The route towards Richmond was resumed at 9 A.M. on the 27th; the army crossed the Pamunkey River at noon on the 28th, and at 9.25 A.M. on the 30th we reached Tolopotomoy Creek, where a large force of the enemy was found in battle array.   The day was spent in getting into position on our front, though there was severe fighting on our left.   About sunset our First Division charged the enemy and was repulsed.   We marched at midnight of June 1st a short distance to the front, to support a charge by the First Brigade, which failed, and next afternoon the march was continued to Cold Harbor, which was reached just before dark, the brigade taking its position in the general line of battle under a steady fire of small-arms.

At daylight next morning another of the famous battles of the great rebellion was fought at this place.   The rebels were advantageously posted and strongly intrenched.   At half-past four o'clock on the morning of the 3d of June the army moved to a general assault.   Our brigade was in the first line deployed, and the Second Brigade was formed

8

in column of battalions about fifty yards in our rear, with instructions to charge right into the rebel works. Through a most destructive fire of artillery and musketry we reached to within seventy-five yards of the rebel fortifications, but the Second Brigade changed its direction to the left of our line and the assault failed. Our men held the position they had gained, however, and gradually intrenched themselves. At 8 P.M. the enemy opened upon us with a tremendous cannonade, followed by a vigorous sortie, which we, in turn, signally repelled, and held our position. After this one-half of the command was kept awake and under arms throughout the remainder of the night. At 10 A.M. First Lieutenant Benjamin Y. Draper, of Company H, serving as an aide to Colonel Smyth, was killed while carrying an order to the front line, and his body was brought to brigade headquarters.

The enemy made another furious attack on our front at half-past ten on the 4th, and was again terribly defeated.

In reference to the attack upon us on the evening of the 3d, General Grant sent a despatch to the War Department, saying, "About 7 P.M. yesterday, Friday, 3d of June, the enemy suddenly attacked Smyth's brigade of Gibbon's division. The battle lasted with great fury for half an hour. The attack was unwaveringly repulsed. Smyth's losses were inconsiderable."

At half-past eight o'clock on the evening of the 5th the rebels made another desperate assault on our brigade, only to meet with the same success as in the former attacks. A truce was agreed upon on the 7th to bury the dead, which lasted from 4 to 8 P.M.

The army quietly withdrew from the trenches at dark on the 12th and marched all night, crossed the Chickahominy River about noon next day, reached Charles City Court-House at night, and encamped.   At noon on the 14th we arrived at the James River, and crossed to Windmill Point in steamboats.   On the 15th we marched rapidly towards Petersburg, and at dark relieved a brigade of the Eighteenth Corps, which had that afternoon captured a strong line of the rebel fortifications, with seventeen guns and about seven hundred prisoners.   It was two o'clock on the morning of the 16th when we got into position.

On the 17th our brigade was ordered to report to General Barlow, commanding the First Division, and took part in an assault on the enemy's line, which resulted in no other advantage than a gain of a hundred or more yards.   Again, at dawn next morning, our division assailed the enemy, drove them a mile and held the ground we took.   We were relieved on the 20th by the Sixth and Ninth Corps, and moved two miles farther to the left.

In the several battles fought after the struggle in the Wilderness the losses in killed among the enlisted men of the regiment were as follows: In the battles at Spottsylvania Court-House those who were killed or died of wounds were, Company B, Privates David S. Riggs, Samuel Creller, and Charles McCullen; Company E, died of wounds, Corporal Robert F. Burrows; Company F, died of wounds, Private William C. Lewis; Company I, killed, Private Edward Rogerson; Company K, killed, Sergeant James Crossley.

In the battle on the North Anna River the only man killed

was Private Jasper Calhoun, of Company A, and at Tolopotomoy Creek the only one killed was Private Gustave A.
Wallace, of Company E.

In the battle of Cold Harbor there were killed Sergeant
William Warren, of Company A; Private Robert Thomas,
of Company B; Corporal Charles P. Prettyman, of Company
E; Private James Mick, of Company F; and Private Hud-
son Carr, of Company I. Died of wounds, Privates David
Guessford, of Company F, and Samuel Alexander, of Company I.

During this time but few changes occurred among the
officers. February 17th, Commissary-Sergeant James Kettlewood was promoted to be first lieutenant of Company
C. March 1st, Sergeant William J. Birney, of Company F,
was appointed commissary-sergeant. April 16th, Sergeant
William H. Ferguson, of Company K, was promoted to
second lieutenant of Company F, and on May 20th he
died of wounds, and on the 21st First Lieutenant James D.
Simpson, of Company D, died of wounds. June 3d, First
Lieutenant Benjamin Y. Draper, of Company H, was killed.

On the morning of the 21st of June the command started
again, and marched to the Jerusalem Plank Road, where we
set to work building intrenchments more in accordance
with the principles of military engineering than were the
rude and hasty breastworks heretofore constructed without
any other guiding rule than chance direction. The enemy,
whose works across the narrow vale that divided them from
us were of quite a substantial character, evidently had re-
solved that we should not effect our lodgment on the
hills opposite, for, on the afternoon of the 22d, they made

a furious charge in masses on the divisions of Generals Barlow and Mott, on our immediate left, and before they could be driven out had captured many of our Second Brigade, with McKnight's battery. Three charges were made before dark to recapture the lost ground, but they all failed, though the rebels were summarily ousted next day. The First Delaware and the Third Brigade did not share in this sudden attack of the enemy, being in the second line, more retired in the wood, but they had their full share of the subsequent fighting in the attempt to recover the lost earthworks.

General Gibbon fell sick on the 24th and Colonel Smyth was assigned to command the division, which honor he enjoyed but a few days. On the 27th the division was relieved from the trenches and sent two or three miles to the rear of the army to meet an expected raid of the enemy's cavalry; they merely skirmished around us enough to find that we were ready and too strong for them. Back to the trenches again on the 29th to relieve a part of the Sixth Corps, which had gone out in support of Wilson's cavalry; they returned, however, on the 2d of July, and we were moved to the right to make room for them.

THE BATTLES AT DEEP BOTTOM.

We were becoming quite comfortable in our spacious trenches, or "gopher-holes," as the men termed them, after a few days' rest, although constantly under fire, when, on the 11th of July, we were astounded by an order to level our breastworks, fill the trenches, and move to the rear. We felt sure that the siege of Petersburg was about to be raised, but we soon found that we were only to act as reserve, do picket duty, and level the fortifications built by the rebels. This duty we continued to perform until the 25th, when marching orders came, with the significant warning to provide three days' cooked rations. This we knew meant serious work. Next day, at half-past three o'clock in the afternoon, the entire corps marched towards City Point, on the James River. The march continued throughout the night, and at daylight on the 27th we crossed James River in steamboats, formed line of battle, and advanced against the enemy at Deep Bottom. We charged their works, captured a battery, and drove the rebels about two miles towards Richmond. At night we intrenched and made every necessary preparation for holding the ground we had taken. On the morning of the 28th our division withdrew from the trenches, and lay in reserve until afternoon, when we were hurried away to the right to support our cavalry, which was getting badly handled by rebel infantry. We attacked the enemy, broke their line, and followed them for nearly a mile; but receiving reinforcements, the rebels made a counter-charge, drove in our skirmish-line, and pounded away at our front until dark, with but little advantage. After night we fell back to a more secure position and went to digging again. Here we waited all day on the 29th, very desirous of having a call from our Confederate friends, but not relishing our hospitable preparations to receive them, they disappointed us; so, after dark, we recrossed the river and executed another night march back to a ravine in the rear of the Ninth Corps, and at daylight witnessed the explosion of the mine, and the disastrous failure to properly support the storming force that charged into the crater. At dark we returned to our former camp. This evening General Gibbon departed on sick-leave, and Colonel Smyth again took command of the division.

A season of rest was allowed the command, which lasted for two weeks, when, on the 12th of August, it was suddenly interrupted by orders to march immediately. At 3 P.M. the Second Corps set out once more for City Point and encamped for the night. At noon on the 13th the troops marched on board of an immense fleet of steamboats and transports with no effort at secrecy, and proceeded some distance down the river for the information of the enemy, but turned about and steamed up the river at 10 P.M. for their discomfiture.

We landed, proceeded to the Newmarket Road, and formed our line for the attack at Strawberry Plains, on Deep Bottom Run. The First Brigade led the assault; gained nothing, but lost heavily. Our attack was made to draw the enemy to our front, while the real attack was made by the Tenth Corps, which carried the enemy's first line, capturing six guns, two mortars, and many prisoners.

On the 16th the Tenth Corps made another assault, took the two remaining lines of the rebel works, but, after five successive charges by the enemy, were compelled to relinquish part of the second line. In the afternoon our brigade was sent to General Birney, to act in support of a division of colored troops. The enemy massed in front of the Tenth Corps on the morning of the 18th, and made a desperate attack to recover lost ground, but met with a terrible defeat. Brisk skirmishing was carried on along our front all day, and at night we moved to the left into the trenches made by Mott's division, our left at the Pottery and our right resting on the Newmarket Road. This position we occupied during the next day, and at night we kept fires burning along a portion of the line where there were no troops to deceive the enemy.

On the night of the 20th the entire detachment returned to the trenches before Petersburg. Next day General Gibbon resumed the command, and we marched to the left of the Jerusalem Plank Road, in support of the Fifth Corps, which had been attacked by the enemy. The battle resulted in a decided repulse for the assailants, and we were held in reserve.

We were marched out again on the 23d, and moved southward on the road to Ream's Station, on the Weldon Railroad, and next day took position at the station, where the First Division went to work tearing up the track. About noon the enemy advanced upon us in heavy force, drove in our skirmishers, made three furious charges on the First Division, the last of which broke our line. Our division was hurried to the support of the First, when the rebels assaulted the line we had just left, and which was held by only a skirmish-line and Gregg's cavalry. These were forced to give way, and our division was sent back on the run to meet this charge of the enemy. We succeeded in arresting the progress of the rebels, and held the line intact; but at this time the rebels opened upon our contracted position (which was something in the form of an irregular letter U) a most destructive fire of artillery and musketry, which lasted for over an hour, and from which the troops were ordered to take such shelter as they could. This, however, was very inadequate, for the long sides of our imperfectly-intrenched position were not more than five hundred yards apart, so that the reverse, or inner side, of each line was exposed to this terrible tornado of missiles. The line was held, nevertheless, excepting a portion of about two hundred yards on the right, which was retained by the enemy. After dark our forces were withdrawn into a small, thick wood at the centre of our position and massed. Before midnight the corps returned to Petersburg, the enemy retiring at the same time and in the same direction.

But one member of the regiment was killed at Ream's Station,—Private Nathan Rash, of Company K. Two others died of wounds received there, however,—Corporal James McIntyre, of Company G, and Private Henry J. Parvis, of Company D. Sergeant John M. Meacham, of Company G, died of wounds received at Deep Bottom on August 15th.

In June, July, and August a few changes took place among the officers. On June 12th Sergeant Theodore Palmatary, of Company F, was made first lieutenant of Company B; on the 18th, Captain J. Parke Postles, of Company A, resigned; on the 27th, Adjutant Charles S. Schaeffer resigned on account of disability; and on the 30th, Second Lieutenant Allen Tatem, of Company H, was discharged. Captain Thomas B. Hizar, of Company I, was appointed on staff duty July 26th, and his brother, Aquila M. Hizar, first lieutenant of Company K, was promoted to captain of Company I, and Commissary-Sergeant William

J. Birney was made first lieutenant of Company D. On August 22d First Lieutenant Theodore Palmatary, of Company B, was appointed adjutant; on the 23d, Sergeant-Major John W. Barney was appointed second lieutenant of Company B; on the 24th, Sergeant Evan P. Grubb, of Company H, was made sergeant-major; and on the 30th, Assistant Surgeon Frederick J. Owens resigned because of disability.

COLONEL SMYTH'S OFFICIAL REPORT.

August 29th, Colonel Smyth rendered his official report of the operations of the Third Brigade, which is as follows:

HEADQUARTERS THIRD BRIGADE, SECOND DIVISION, SECOND CORPS.

IN THE FIELD, August 29, 1864.

CAPTAIN A. H. EMBLER, A.A.A.G.

CAPTAIN,—I have the honor to submit the following report of the operations of the Third Brigade, Second Division, Second Corps, from May 17, 1864, the date upon which I assumed command, to July 30, 1864, divided into four epochs, pursuant to Special Order No. 209, Headquarters of the Army of the Potomac:

First.—I assumed command of this brigade by order of Brigadier-General Gibbon, May 17, 1864, the army then being in the vicinity of Spottsylvania Court-House. About 8.30 P.M. I was ordered to mass the brigade in front of the Landrum House, and near the vacated line of the enemy's intrenchments, before daylight, which was accomplished, the brigade being in column of battalions between the Landrum House and the road. Subsequently it was deployed into line by battalions in mass, and I was ordered by Brigadier-General Gibbon to move forward in support of the Corcoran Legion.

At daylight the Legion moved forward, and I followed at a short supporting distance. The first line was repulsed, and my brigade, taking position in a ravine, covered their retreat. I at once deployed a line of skirmishers, and held this position until 12.35 P.M., when, in obedience to orders from General

Gibbon, I withdrew to the second line of intrenchments, where my command formed line of battle and rested. At 10 P.M. the brigade moved to Anderson's Mills, where it took position. On the morning of May 19th the command went into camp, the First Delaware Volunteers being detailed for picket. At 6 P.M. an order was received for the brigade to march at once. The brigade moved quickly to the Fredericksburg Road. The order was soon countermanded, and the command returned to camp at Anderson's Mills.

Second.—May 20th I received an order to move with my command at 11 P.M. I moved at 11.20 P.M., taking the road towards Mattapony Church, continuing the marching May 21st, passing Grimes' Station, passing through Milford and Bowling Green, etc., crossing the Ny River, where the command went into position and threw up intrenchments, the Eighth Ohio Volunteers being detailed for picket.

May 22d I received orders from General Gibbon to take my brigade and make a reconnoissance to develop the strength and position of the enemy. The regiments composing the force were the Fourteenth Connecticut, Seventh Virginia, Fourteenth Indiana, Tenth New York, Twelfth New Jersey, and Fourth Ohio Volunteers. The First Delaware and One Hundred and Eighth New York Volunteers were employed in erecting earth-works. I deployed the Fourteenth Indiana and Fourth Ohio Volunteers as skirmishers. One lieutenant and twenty men of the Tenth New York Volunteers were placed on the right and rear of the skirmish-line to protect that flank, and two companies of the Fourteenth Connecticut Volunteers were similarly placed to protect the left flank.

Colonel T. G. Ellis, Fourteenth Connecticut Volunteers, and Lieutenant-Colonel Carpenter, Fourth Ohio Volunteers, were assigned respectively to the command of the left and right wings of the skirmish-line. Two companies of the Fourteenth Connecticut Volunteers were sent to reconnoitre the Hanover Junction Road. The Twelfth New Jersey and Tenth New York Volunteers were placed in support of artillery near the cross-roads, and the Seventh Virginia stationed near the cross-roads. The skirmish-line was then pushed forward about two miles, finding nothing but cavalry or mounted infantry to oppose them.

About 3 P.M. I received orders from General Gibbon to halt, and I was subsequently ordered to assemble my command and return to camp. On

May 23d the command marched, at 7 A.M., to the North Anna River, where the enemy was discovered to be posted in force. At noon my brigade was massed behind a ridge of hills. At 4 P.M. the Fourth Ohio Volunteers was deployed as skirmishers, and moved to the river-bank, where it became engaged at once with the enemy on the opposite shore. It was relieved at dark by the Seventh Virginia Volunteers. At 7 P.M. I was ordered by General Gibbon to make a demonstration against the railroad bridge across the river. I moved the Eighth Ohio and Fourteenth Indiana Volunteers to the bridge, where they opened fire on the enemy's skirmishers. During the night my brigade intrenched itself.

Shortly after midnight the enemy succeeded in burning the bridge. At 7 A.M., May 24th, I received an order from General Gibbon to construct a rough bridge and cross a regiment as skirmishers. About 10.15 A.M. the bridge was completed, and the Eighth Ohio Volunteers moved to the opposite side, deployed and advanced to the enemy's earth-works, which they occupied, the enemy having fallen back. The remainder of the brigade was then crossed and took position in line of battle. At 3 P.M. I was ordered to advance and ascertain the position of the enemy. The First Delaware and One Hundred and Eighth New York Volunteers were deployed as skirmishers, and advanced about half a mile, the left swinging forward. At this point the enemy offered a strong resistance, and I deployed the Fourteenth Connecticut Volunteers to strengthen the line. I then moved forward again, but, as the enemy were posted in rifle-pits, in the edge of a wood, while my skirmishers were obliged to pass on an elevated ploughed field, the line was again brought to a halt. I then addressed the Twelfth New Jersey Volunteers to charge the enemy's rifle-pits, which was done in fine style, the enemy being driven about five hundred yards. The enemy having been reinforced, I brought up the Seventh Virginia and Tenth New York Volunteers to strengthen the left centre of my line. The pressure still continuing strongest at this point, and the Nineteenth Maine Volunteers having reported to me, I ordered it also to that part of the line.

Learning that the enemy was moving troops towards my right, I directed the Eighth Ohio, Fourth Ohio, and Fourteenth Indiana Volunteers to take position to cover the right flank of my line of battle. At 5.30 P.M. the enemy made a determined attack on my centre.

The Sixty-ninth and One Hundred and Seventieth New York Volunteers, which had reported to me, were brought in to strengthen this part of the line, and the Fourth Ohio, Eighth Ohio, and Fourteenth Indiana Volunteers were moved from the right to the centre. This attack of the enemy was handsomely repulsed. The Fifteenth and Nineteenth Massachusetts Volunteers having reported to me, I directed them to form on the right, relieving the Twelfth New Jersey, First Delaware, One Hundred and Eighth New York, and Seventh Virginia Volunteers, which regiments were formed in the rear and resupplied with ammunition. The Sixty-ninth Pennsylvania Volunteers reporting to me at this time, was formed on the left of my line of battle.

Just at dark a vigorous attack was made by the enemy on my left, which threw the Sixty-ninth and One Hundred and Seventieth New York Volunteers into considerable disorder, which resulted in their falling back. I succeeded in rallying them, however, and formed that part of the line at right angles with the main line. During the night my command threw up intrenchments. On the morning of the 25th the first line was pushed forward with but little opposition, and, on the right, breastworks were erected in advance of the previous position. The first line now consisted, from right to left, of the Seventh Virginia, One Hundred and Eighth New York, First Delaware, Eighth Ohio, Twelfth New Jersey, Fourteenth Connecticut, Sixty-ninth Pennsylvania, and One Hundred and Seventieth New York Volunteers. The Fourth Ohio, Fourteenth Indiana, and Tenth New York Volunteers were in the second line. At dark the Fourth Ohio and Fourteenth Indiana Volunteers were moved by me to the Doswell House to cover the left flank of my position. At 5 P.M., May 26th, I received orders from General Gibbon to advance my skirmish-line by swinging forward the left, and to dislodge a force of the enemy who held a salient near the left of my line. At dark I pushed forward the Sixty-ninth Pennsylvania, One Hundred and Seventieth New York, and two companies of the Fourteenth Connecticut Volunteers, who charged the enemy and drove him from his position. Soon after I received an order from General Gibbon to be prepared to recross the North Anna. At 8 P.M. the brigade moved across the river and bivouacked until morning.

Third.—On May 27th the command marched to within a mile of Haunquartus Creek, where it bivouacked for the night. At noon, May 28th, we crossed the Pamunkey River. At 1 P.M. I received an order to follow the cavalry, which was subsequently countermanded, and my brigade filed into the field on the left of the road and took position in two lines of battle. On May 29th I was directed to swing forward the left of my command, move about half a mile to the front, form line of battle, and intrench. Subsequently I was ordered to hold the command in readiness to march at short notice. At 5.30 A.M., May 30th, the command marched, acting as a reserve. At 9.25 A.M. I was ordered to move farther to the front. My brigade was then formed in line of battle near the Jones House. The Seventh Virginia Volunteers was directed to drive the enemy's sharpshooters from a house about five hundred yards in front of my left flank, which they quickly accomplished. On May 31st I received orders to be in readiness to support the First Brigade. At 1 P.M. the command was marched across Tolopotomoy Creek and massed in rear of the First Brigade. At 2 P.M. the One Hundred and Eighth New York and Seventh Virginia Volunteers were sent to the support of the right.

At dark the Fourteenth Connecticut, Eighth Ohio, and Twelfth New Jersey Volunteers were formed in an interval between the First and Second Brigades. Soon after dark the Eighth Ohio Volunteers was relieved and returned to its original position. At 12.25 P.M., June 1st, I was ordered by General Gibbon to be in readiness to march at once. This order was subsequently countermanded, and the brigade threw up intrenchments. At dark I was directed to occupy the earth-works and relieve the First Brigade. At 9 P.M. the brigade marched, taking the road to Cold Harbor, which place it reached June 2d. At 2.20 P.M., June 2d, my brigade was deployed in line of battle, and, by order of General Gibbon, advanced to a vacated line of rifle-pits, where it took position under a severe fire from the enemy's skirmishers, who were concealed in rifle-pits, within short range of my right. At 5 P.M. I was ordered to attack the enemy's position, but the attack was subsequently deferred. The One Hundred and Eighty-fourth Pennsylvania Volunteers reported to me, and was placed on the extreme right of my line. During the night sharp skirmishing occurred on my right. At 4.30 A.M., June 3d, I was ordered to attack the enemy. I formed my brigade in line of battle, and at 4.30 A.M. advanced and charged the enemy's works. When the command arrived at from sixty to one hundred yards from the enemy's works the ranks became so thinned, and the fire from the enemy's artillery and musketry was so destructive, that the men were compelled to halt and seek such shelter as presented itself. In this position the command soon erected a rude breastwork. At 9 A.M. Berdan's Sharpshooters and a battalion of the First Massachusetts Heavy Artillery reported to me. I deployed part of the Sharpshooters in front as skirmishers, and held the battalion of First Massachusetts Heavy Artillery in reserve. At 4 P.M. the One Hundred and Sixty-fourth New York Volunteers and the remaining battalion of the First Massachusetts Heavy Artillery reported to me, which regiments I formed on the opposite side of the ravine, on my extreme right. My line strengthened their works, and was arranged from right to left, as follows: First Massachusetts Heavy Artillery, One Hundred and Sixty-fourth New York, Fourteenth Connecticut, Eighth Ohio, Fourth Ohio, Seventh Virginia, Twelfth New Jersey, Tenth New York, First Delaware, and Fourteenth Indiana.

About 8 P.M. the enemy opened upon us a terrible artillery fire, which lasted about thirty minutes, after which they charged along my whole line. They were repulsed with considerable loss. During the night one-half the command was kept awake and under arms. In this action Lieutenant Benjamin Y. Draper, A.A.D.C., on my staff, a brave and gallant young officer, was killed. At 10.30 A.M., June 4th, the enemy opened on us a heavy artillery fire, which continued until 11.35, doing but little injury. Sharp skirmishing was kept up all day. At 8.40 P.M. the brisk skirmish changed to a very heavy musketry fire on both sides, followed by a short artillery duel, which did no damage to my brigade except the wounding of one of my staff orderlies, Private James Kay, Tenth New York Volunteers. Severe skirmishing continued all day. June 5th, in the afternoon, my standard-bearer, Private Elliott, Tenth New York Volunteers, was mortally wounded whilst carrying an order.

At 8.30 P.M. the enemy commenced a vigorous attack with artillery and musketry, which lasted twenty-four minutes, without doing injury. Heavy skirmishing continued during June 6th, and until 4 P.M., June 7th, when a cessation of hostilities was ordered to give opportunity to bury the dead. During the 8th and 9th of June there was very little skirmishing, and on the 10th my command was relieved from duty in the intrenchments. There was skirmishing all day June 11th. At dark, June 12th, the command marched to the left.

Fourth.—The brigade marched all day June 13th, and encamped near Wilcox's Landing, on James River. About dark, June 14th, we crossed James River on transports and encamped at Windmill Point. At 10.30 A.M.,

June 15th, the brigade moved towards Petersburg, and, about 10 P.M., relieved the troops of the Eighteenth Army Corps. Skirmishing during the 16th.

On June 17th I was ordered to report with my command to General Barlow. On June 18th I took position at daylight, and at 4 A.M. advanced upon the enemy's position, and discovered that he had fallen back about half a mile. During the day the brigade charged twice. After skirmishing during the 19th and 20th the command was relieved, and marched to the left about three miles and encamped. At 8 A.M., June 21st, the brigade marched, and took position on the left of the Jerusalem Plank Road, where the enemy was found intrenched. In this position we threw up breastworks.

At 3 P.M., June 22d, the enemy attacked the troops on our left, turned the flank of the first line, and captured a battery and many prisoners. On the 23d the enemy vacated the line of works they had captured. On June 24th my command moved to the rear and relieved some of the Fifth Corps. We remained in this position until June 27th, when the brigade was deployed to picket the rear of the army, remaining on picket until June 29th, when I was ordered to move to the intrenchments of the Sixth Corps.

On July 2d the command moved to the right, and on the 11th commenced tearing down the breastworks in front of them. On July 12th my brigade was on picket, and continued on that duty until the morning of July 15th, when they were relieved by troops of the Fifth Corps, and went into the rear of the Southall House. In the evening of the 15th the command marched to Haines's House, and commenced to tear down the old rebel works in the vicinity, returning to camp on the morning of the 16th. The brigade remained in camp until July 21st, when they were set to work making a covered way in the rear of the Fifth Corps' intrenchments.

On July 22d the brigade moved into the intrenchments previously occupied by Ferrero's division of colored troops, remaining in these works until July 26th, when, at 3.30 P.M., the command was massed near corps headquarters, and at 4.25 moved off towards the Appomattox, which river we crossed on pontoons during the night. At daylight on the 27th the brigade crossed the James River, and were soon engaged in skirmishing with the enemy. On July 28th my command marched to support the cavalry, and at dark took up a new position and intrenched. During the night of the 29th we marched back to the vicinity of Petersburg, and at daylight were massed in the rear of the Fifth Corps. After the explosion of the mine and the failure of the assault on the enemy's works, the command returned to camp near the Southall House.

The loss of the brigade during the campaign, including the battle of the Wilderness, when Colonel Carroll was in command, is as follows:

Commissioned officers killed	22
" " wounded	72
" " missing	9
Enlisted men killed	254
" " wounded	1320
" " missing	278

Total number of casualties.

Commissioned officers	103
Enlisted men	1852
Grand total	1955

The conduct of both officers and men during the campaign has been in every respect unexceptionable. It is a source of extreme gratification to me to be able to recommend to the major-general commanding the division the gentlemen of my staff for the prompt and efficient manner in which they executed all my orders. Their gallantry on the field of battle has seldom been surpassed.

Very respectfully, your obedient servant,

THOMAS A. SMYTH,

Colonel Commanding Third Brigade, Second Division, Second Army Corps.

At 10 A.M. on the 26th we marched from Ream's Station to the Williams House, where we encamped. The loss of the division in the battle of Ream's Station was eleven hundred and seventy-eight.

THE FALL OF RICHMOND AND PETERSBURG.

Moved again on the 30th to the trenches, where the brigade was placed in the third line of breastworks. September 4th, General Gibbon was ordered to take temporary command of the Eighteenth Army Corps, and Colonel Smyth once more took command of the division.

The enemy opened upon our front with shot and shell at 3.30 P.M., and in the midst of this attack the division was moved in rear of the Jones House and put to work throwing up intrenchments. At this work we were kept, marching and digging, until the 16th, when considerable alarm was created by a sudden raid of the rebel cavalry upon the rear of our army and the capture of twenty-five hundred cattle. Our division was hastened off to Prince George's Court-House, where the Third Brigade was left to guard the rear, accompanied by Ames' battery. Thus matters stood until the 24th, when we were ordered to the front again, to relieve the Tenth Corps in the trenches, and our line occupied from the Norfolk Railroad on the left to Battery No. 13 on the right. Here we were under an almost constant skirmish fire, frequently aggravated by cannonading at very short range; but we were well covered by earth-works. General Gibbon relieved Colonel Smyth, and resumed the command on the 25th.

On the 28th orders were received to leave the garrisons in the forts on our front, and, with the rest of the men, march at 4 A.M. next morning. At the appointed hour the command was ready, but no further orders were received until October 1st, at which time we were moved once more to the front, and relieved General Mott's division.

Colonel Thomas A. Smyth received his promotion to the rank of brigadier-general on the 4th of October, and was the recipient of many ceremonial calls and much congratulation. October 6th we moved to the right, and occupied the works from Fort Sedgwick to Fort Morton. For more than two weeks the brigade was employed in defending the outer line of intrenchments.

The officers of the brigade had with great secrecy made up a purse of about twelve hundred dollars, and had despatched a messenger to Washington to procure a mounted outfit as a present to General Smyth; and the officers and men of the First Delaware had purchased for him a fine horse. On the morning of the 22d General Smyth was induced to go out for a ride, and in his absence the presents were brought to his tent. They consisted of a saddle, saddle-cloth, saddle-bags, holsters, bridle and martingale, belt, sword, sash, and shoulder-straps. The horse was saddled and the other articles arranged about the tent. Shortly after everything was fully prepared for the ceremony of presentation, the general returned, and was amazed to see the vast concourse that was gathered about his headquarters. He was highly gratified with this manifestation of the esteem in which he was held by his comrades in arms, and expressed his thanks warmly and gracefully.

On the 25th orders came to withdraw from the trenches and mass the command in the rear, and on the morning of the 26th the entire corps marched to the left, crossing the Weldon Railroad, and at night bivouacked near Gravelly Run, the First Delaware being thrown to the front to furnish a picket-line.

The command had hardly commenced a forward movement on the morning of the 27th, when they met the enemy near the Boydton Plank Road, prepared to dispute the way. The battle opened at once hot and furious, and our brigade came in for a liberal share of the hard fighting; but, though the destruction of life was very great on both sides, the engagement was of short duration, the enemy finally giving way and opening the road to our troops.

In this battle the regiment lost one of its best officers, Major William F. Smith, who was mortally wounded while leading the regiment to engage the rebel line, he being in command. He died of his wounds on the 11th of November.

Colonel Smyth's diary furnishes an account of this action, from which the following extract is taken:

" Orders to march at 3 A.M., my brigade in advance; rode with a squad of cavalry, leading; surprised and drove the rebel vedettes in. At Cedar Creek we were checked by a strong force of rebs. My brigade formed in line of battle and charged, wading the creek to their arm-pits, and carried the works in fine style, pushing the enemy and advancing in good order. After crossing the open field, we halted the command and formed the line again, putting the First Delaware out as skirmishers, who advanced and drove the enemy three-fourths of a mile. We then took the road to Anderson's Mills, the First Brigade in advance. Were put in position by Major-General Hancock, and deployed the fourth company of the Fourteenth Connecticut as skirmishers, and charged a battery, which limbered up and left. I soon after received orders to support the Second Brigade, and advance to the mill on the right of the road. Orders to form on right of Second Brigade, and while performing this movement the rebels advanced and drove the cavalry back. I ordered the First Delaware by the left flank and charged the rebel line, following them to the creek and taking their works. This position I held all day, subject to a fire from all flanks."

This last charge was led by General Smyth in person.

With this battle ended the active campaigning of the year 1864. During the winter the troops were employed in skirmishing, and in gradually extending our line of earth-works farther to the left. Before the close of the year General Hancock left the Army of the Potomac to take command of the First Veteran Corps, and General Humphreys was placed in command of the Second Corps. General John Gibbon was assigned to command the Twenty-fourth Army Corps, and General Smyth took command of the division.

While encamped here in winter quarters several changes occurred in the regiment. September 4th, Second Lieutenant John W. Barney, of Company B, was advanced to first lieutenant; on the 10th, Sergeant Louis J. M. Pennington, of Company I, was appointed commissary-sergeant; on the 15th, Sergeant William Caywood, of Company A, was promoted to first lieutenant of Company H; First Lieutenant John W. Eckles, of Company I, was discharged on expiration of service, and First Lieutenant Henry G. Cavanaugh, of Company H, was transferred to Company I; on the 24th, Hospital Steward Archibald D. O'Mera was discharged on expiration of enlistment, as was also First Lieutenant James Kettlewood, of Company C.

October 2d, Sergeant Joseph E. Booth, of Company H, was appointed hospital steward, and Sergeant Emanuel W. Hilt, of Company C, was made second lieutenant of that company; on the 5th, Captain Ezekiel C. Alexander, of Company C, was discharged at the close of his term of service; and on the 8th, Captain Aquila M. Hizar, of Company I, and First Lieutenant John L. Brady, of Company E, were discharged for the same reason. On the same day Second Lieutenant Charles W. Davis, of Company G, was made first lieutenant of Company E, Quartermaster-Sergeant James M. Bryan was made second lieutenant of Company A, and John G. Raymond, who had been transferred from the Second Delaware Regiment, was appointed quartermaster-sergeant. On the 11th of October Captain William P. Seville, of Company E, was discharged on expiration of service.

On October 26th Captain J. M. Wenie, from the Second Delaware Volunteers, was assigned to the command of Company A.

On November 10th Sergeant-Major Evan P. Grubb was made first lieutenant of Company K, and Sergeant James H. Barbour, of Company K, was appointed sergeant-major; on the 11th, Major William F. Smith died of wounds; on the 17th, Captain Joseph C. Nicholls, of Company B, was promoted to major; First Lieutenant Charles W. Davis, of Company E, was advanced to captain; and Sergeant John M. Dunn, of Company K, was promoted to first lieutenant of that company on the 20th; on the 24th, First Lieutenant Washington F. Williamson, of Company A, was discharged at the close of his service.

December 23d, Lieutenant-Colonel Daniel Woodall was promoted to colonel, and on the 26th Major Nicholls was again raised, to the rank of lieutenant-colonel; First Lieutenant Henry G. Cavanaugh, of Company I, was made captain; Second Lieutenant Emanuel W. Hilt, of Company C, was made first lieutenant; Sergeant-Major James H. Barbour was made first lieutenant of Company I; Hospital Steward Joseph E. Booth was promoted to second lieutenant of Company B; Sergeant W. N. Meacham was pro-

moted to second lieutenant of Company G; and Sergeant
W. Murphey, of Company F, to second lieutenant of his
company.

The extension of our lines of circumvallation to the left
was continued at intervals through January and February,
1865; and on the 5th of February our left was near Hatcher's Run. Here the enemy showed a decided disposition to
put a stop to further encroachments. Early on the morning of the 5th the Second Corps set out to feel the way
still farther to the left, the enemy making fierce attacks at
intervals throughout the day. Of the movements of this
and the day following General Smyth's diary contains
these notes:

"On the 5th, at 7 A.M., we took up our line of march, First, Second, and
Third Brigades. Three hundred cavalry reported to me, and the Tenth New
York Battery. We took the road to Armstrong's Mills, driving the enemy's
vedettes and skirmishers across Hatcher's Run. I took up position with my
left resting on the run and right on the swamp, with the Twentieth Massachusetts and Sixty-ninth Pennsylvania Volunteers on the right. The enemy
opened several times through the day with artillery, but we did not reply to
them. In the afternoon, at 4.30, they made a fierce attack on the Twentieth
Massachusetts and Sixty-ninth Pennsylvania, driving them in; the Third Brigade of the Third Division formed in their rear, with the Twelfth New Jersey;
the attack was gallantly repulsed.

"February 6th, at 4 P.M., the Fifth Corps made a reconnoissance to Burgess's
mill, and, after a sharp fire of musketry, they fell back to their old position,
followed closely by the enemy, when my left became engaged. Smyth's battery
did good execution."

In regard to this series of actions, General Humphreys,
in general orders, said, "The enemy concentrated a powerful force, composed of parts of two corps (Hill's and Gor-

don's), on the right of Smyth, Murphy's brigade, and the artillery, and in front of McAllister, and made a determined effort to break our line. They were skilfully and gallantly met, and repulsed with severe loss to them and slight to us."

Then followed what was, comparatively speaking, a long rest for the command, lasting from February 7th until March 25th, during which little more was done than keeping the enemy in a continual shiver of apprehension with unexpected gusts of skirmishing and mysterious movements of bodies of troops. As the roads were now dry, and the weather quite favorable for active operations, the order to march on the 25th of the month was generally anticipated.

Early on the morning of the 25th of March the order to be in readiness to move was received, and in the afternoon our brigade, led by General Smyth, assaulted the rebel works and carried a part of them, capturing a large number of prisoners. At this time General William Hays, of the regular army, was assigned to the command of the division, and General Smyth resumed command of the brigade.

At 6 A.M. on the 29th the command stretched out on the Vaughn Road, and after marching a short distance formed in line on the right of that road. On the morning of the 30th a general advance was made against the enemy's position, the Third Brigade being held in reserve. The rebels offered little opposition, but fell back beyond Hatcher's Run. Shortly after midnight the brigade moved farther to the left and took position in the rear of McAllister's brigade. The battle opened at early daylight on the left, in an effort to obtain possession of the White Oak Road. The Fifth Corps assaulted, and was pressed back towards the Second Corps, which also gave way for some distance on the left. At 11 A.M. our line advanced to relieve the pressure on the Fifth Corps. The men charged gallantly, capturing the first lines of rifle-pits, and drove the enemy to their main works, but failed to carry these, owing to their great natural strength and the obstructions placed in the way. In the evening the brigade fell back to the road. The diversion in favor of the forces on the left enabled them, however, to drive the enemy in turn, and resulted in securing possession of the White Oak Road.

The gallantry of Major John T. Dent, who commanded the regiment in this engagement, contributed largely to the success of the day. The charge of the regiment upon the rifle-pits of the enemy, driving the rebels out and far beyond them, added fresh laurels to its well-earned reputation for warlike prowess. In this bold charge, Major Dent was ably supported by Captain Charles W. Davis, of Company E, and Captain James Kettlewood, of Company H.

April 1st the brigade was ordered to report to General G. E. Mott, but, before proceeding far, was ordered back to its old position as a reserve. This afternoon General Sheridan and the Fifth Corps captured an important work of the enemy, with many guns and over five thousand prisoners. It was a cheering spectacle to us, this full division of the enemy, as they passed through our camp on their way to the rear, for it gave promise of the rapid disintegration of the rebel army and of the near prospect of peace and rest. Certainly the Rebellion was nearing its "last ditch,"—a few more gasps and the dying cause would be forever lost.

On the morning of the 2d orders came to charge the enemy's works again at four o'clock, and every disposition was made to carry the order into effect, but before the time arrived it was changed, and the brigade was again instructed to report to General Mott. The reason the order to charge was countermanded was that during the night the enemy on our front had deserted their works and retreated towards Petersburg. In the afternoon the division moved to the left on the Fox Hill Road, to unite with Sheridan's force, halting at night on the South Side Railroad.

Orders were received during the night to return to Petersburg in the morning, which were changed, however, and the entire command started off at 11.30 A.M. on the road towards Lynchburg instead. Here we learned that the rebels had evacuated Petersburg, and that Richmond had at last fallen, and the enemy was marching rapidly in the direction of Danville. The brigade went into bivouac late at night, started again next morning, finally moving into position near the Danville Railroad, subsequently changing position to the left of the Fifth Corps at Jetersville Station.

In order to reach the bridge over the Appomattox in time to prevent its destruction by the enemy, it was necessary to make a long and a forced march. The First Delaware was near the head of the column to which was intrusted this difficult enterprise, and the duty was fully and successfully executed.

During this march considerable merriment was indulged in at the expense of Lieutenant John M. Dunn, of Company

E. Lieutenant Dunn seemed very desirous of knowing the distance to the Danville Railroad, and made so many inquiries in regard to it that the matter became somewhat of a joke to several of the officers, among them Captain John W. Barney, of Company B. At length an aged negro was seen by the roadside.

"Now, then," said Lieutenant Dunn, "you fellows may laugh, but I am going to find out how far it is to the Danville Road."

When they reached the old negro, the lieutenant asked him the well-worn question, and, by the look of deep wisdom that lit up the old man's face, they saw at once that they had found one who could give them the desired information.

"De Danville Railroad," said he. "Yes, sah! Hit's jes' fo' miles f'm John Thompson's, sah."

For the rest of the day there was not much peace for Lieutenant Dunn; and next day, when the troops had attacked the enemy at High Bridge, charged across the bridge through a perfect tornado of shot, and were reforming under a brisk fire on the other side, Captain Barney shouted to Lieutenant Dunn, "I say, Dunn, how far is it to the Danville Railroad?"

Marched again at 5 A.M. on the 6th, under orders to assault the enemy's works. The route lay along the High Bridge road, reaching High Bridge about eight o'clock in the morning. The rebels were posted here in strong force and disputed the passage of the stream with great stubbornness, setting the bridge on fire; but we succeeded, by an effort of great daring, in taking the bridge in time to save it from destruction, thus preventing much delay in crossing the Appomattox, and increasing the pressure on the already demoralized rebel rear-guard.

In this gallant charge across the railroad bridge, Lieutenant John M. Dunn, in command of Company G, rendered important service in leading the assault. General Barlow was urging the troops that had reached the end of the bridge to charge through the carriage-way beneath the railroad track, which was defended at the other end by the enemy with artillery and musketry, and there was some hesitation about taking the lead, when a part of our regiment supporting the skirmish-line arrived on the spot. Seeing the reluctance to enter the bridge, Lieutenant Dunn asked Lieutenant-Colonel Nicholls if he should take his company and charge across the bridge, at which General Barlow said, "Yes, lieutenant, I wish you would." Company G at once plunged into the bridge, led by the lieutenant, and followed by many others of the First Delaware and other troops. The charge was successful, and the bridge was saved, though at the sacrifice of many brave men, for the fire that swept it was terrible. For this gallant deed Lieutenant Dunn and the noble company which he temporarily commanded were highly complimented by General Barlow and Lieutenant-Colonel Nicholls.

The charge upon the enemy holding the bridge was made just in time to defeat their attempt to destroy this important means of reaching the farther side of the river; and the bridge once in our possession, the entire Union army hastened across and recommenced with vigor the pursuit of the flying enemy towards the town of Farmville, capturing several guns, which, in their hasty retreat, they yielded with but feeble resistance.

It was in the engagement that took place near Farmville that General Thomas A. Smyth received his mortal wound. The occurrence is described by Dr. D. W. Maull, in " The Life and Military Services of the late Brigadier-General Thomas A. Smyth," in the following words :

" A short distance from that town our forces had been temporarily checked by the heavy fire from the rebel artillery and sharpshooters. The general was in advance, with the skirmish-line, as was his frequent custom, as he always wished to form an intelligent conception as to what was transpiring. He was mounted, with his staff about him. It was now about eleven o'clock in the morning, with a cold, disagreeable rain falling. There was an irregular fire of musketry going on. Suddenly he was seen to fall on the right side of his horse. His staff quickly dismounted and caught him. He was laid down, and it was discovered that he had been hit by a rebel sharpshooter. A small conical ball had entered the left side of his face, about an inch from the mouth, cutting away a tooth. The ball continued its course to the neck, fracturing a cervical vertebra, and driving a fragment of the bone upon the spinal cord. Entire paralysis resulted. He was at once placed upon a stretcher and tenderly moved by a relay of sorrowing men to a farm-house in the vicinity, where the corps hospital was established, and where he received all the attention possible."

Next day he was sent in an ambulance to Burkesville Station, accompanied by two of his aides (Lieutenants Tanner and Nones), but, as it was found that he was growing worse, he was taken to the residence of Colonel Burke, where, at 4 A.M. on the 9th, he died. His body was embalmed at Burkesville and forwarded to Wilmington for burial. Thus passed away a noble man, an able soldier, and a loved comrade of the regiment, on the very day that witnessed the surrender of the main army of the Confederacy; he being the last general officer killed on the Union side.

Surgeon Maull was constantly in attendance on the wounded general, and all that the highest surgical skill could accomplish was done to relieve from pain his passage to the shadowy shore, for the character of the wound was fatal beyond all doubt. For his tender devotion on this among numerous other occasions, Surgeon Maull won the highest respect and affection of the men of the regiment, as he did the esteem of all those of the division who had need of his professional aid while he was surgeon-in-chief of the division. His conscientious devotion to his duties, his prompt willingness to sacrifice his own personal ease and comfort to relieve suffering, the earnestness with which he studied every case which came under his care, his extended knowledge of prophylactics and therapeutics, his gentle manner and sympathizing voice, together with his genial social qualities, all combined to make him what our men, with much pride, pronounced a very model of an army surgeon.

The following extract from General Smyth's diary is the last entry made by him:

"April 2d I received orders to assault the enemy's works at 4 o'clock A.M. Three o'clock orders countermanded: orders to report to General Mott. Heavy artillery and musketry along the line all night. The enemy left the works at ten o'clock; marched to near Petersburg. At two o'clock took the Fox Hill Road to Sheridan and the Fifth Corps; bivouacked on the South Side Road. April 3d, orders to return towards Petersburg at sunrise; remained until 11.30, and then took the road towards Lynchburg; at 10 P.M. bivouacked. April 4th, orders to march at 6 A.M.; took up our line of march at seven.   April 5th, at eight o'clock took up the march for the Danville Railroad, and took up position at the left of the Fifth Corps, at Jetersville Station.   April 6th, orders to march at 5 A.M., and at six o'clock to assault the enemy's works."

While the regiment was deployed as skirmishers at Farmville, and was pressing the enemy hard, Colonel Daniel Woodall and Lieutenant-Colonel Joseph C. Nicholls rode in advance of the left wing, and their cool and energetic behavior afforded a fine example to the command.   It was during this advance that Lieutenant-Colonel Nicholls was severely wounded in the face by a piece of shell, and Colonel Woodall's horse was shot.

Lieutenant-Colonel Nicholls and Major Dent both reached their exalted stations in the regiment by promotion from the ranks, owing to their bravery and efficiency as commanders, and both were great favorites with their comrades.

The command marched with the corps to the vicinity of Appomattox Station, but the only fighting that occurred was on the morning of the 9th, in General Sheridan's front, brought on by the enemy making a desperate attempt to break through the cavalry by charging with masses of infantry.   General Ord's division arrived in time, however, to defeat their object, and overtures were immediately made by the enemy looking to surrender.   Negotiations were soon completed, and the Army of Northern Virginia, commanded by General Robert E. Lee, surrendered on that day, thus virtually closing the war and ending the great Rebellion.

THE SURRENDER OF LEE.

As the movements of the two opposing forces and the negotiations for surrender at Appomattox Court-House will ever be one of the brightest pages in the history of the war, and as it is a fitting and satisfactory close of the service for which the First Delaware Regiment had volunteered, an extract from the official report of Lieutenant-General Grant is added here, that these valuable papers bearing upon the history of the nation may form a part (as of right they should) of the history of our regiment.

Referring to the rapid concentration of our forces near Farmville on the 7th of April, and the failure of Lee to preserve a road on which to escape the toils by which he was surrounded, General Grant says:

" Feeling now that General Lee's chance of escape was utterly hopeless, I addressed him the following communication from Farmville:

" ' April 7, 1865.

" ' GENERAL,—The result of the last week must convince you of the hopelessness of further resistance on the part of the Army of Northern Virginia in this struggle. I feel that it is so, and regard it as my duty to shift from myself the responsibility of any further effusion of blood by asking of you the surrender of that portion of the Confederate States army known as the Army of Northern Virginia.

" ' U. S. GRANT, *Lieutenant-General.*
" ' GENERAL R. E. LEE.'

" Early on the morning of the 8th, before leaving, I received, at Farmville, the following:

" ' ———, 1865.

" ' GENERAL,—I have received your note of this day. Though not entertaining the opinion you express on the hopelessness of further resistance on the part of the Army of Northern Virginia, I reciprocate your desire to avoid useless effusion of blood, and therefore, before considering your proposition, ask the terms you will offer on condition of its surrender.

" 'R. E. Lee, General.

" ' Lieutenant-General U. S. Grant.'

" To this I immediately replied :

" 'April 8, 1865.

" ' General,—Your note of last evening, in reply to mine of the same date, asking the conditions on which I will accept the surrender of the Army of Northern Virginia, is just received. In reply I would say that *peace* being my great desire, there is but one condition I would insist upon,—namely, that the men and officers surrendered shall be disqualified for taking up arms against the government of the United States until properly exchanged. I will meet you, or will designate officers to meet any officers you may name for the same purpose, at any point agreeable to you, for the purpose of arranging definitely the terms upon which the surrender of the Army of Northern Virginia will be received.

" ' U. S. Grant, Lieutenant-General.

" ' General R. E. Lee.'

" Early on the morning of the 8th the pursuit was resumed. General Meade followed on the north of the Appomattox, and General Sheridan, with all the cavalry, pushed straight for Appomattox Station, followed by General Ord's command and the Fifth Corps. During the day General Meade's advance had considerable fighting with the enemy's rear-guard, but was unable to bring on a general engagement. Late in the evening General Sheridan struck the railroad at Appomattox Station, drove the enemy from there, and captured twenty-five pieces of artillery, a hospital-train, and five trains of cars loaded with supplies for Lee's army. During this day I accompanied General Meade's column, and about midnight received the following communication from General Lee :

" 'April 8, 1865.

" ' General,—I received at a late hour your note of to-day. In mine of yesterday I did not intend to propose the surrender of the Army of Northern Virginia, but to ask the terms of your proposition. To be frank, I do not think the emergency has arisen to call for the surrender of this army, but as the restoration of peace should be the sole object of all, I desire to know whether your proposal would lead to that end.   I cannot, therefore, meet you with a view to surrender the Army of Northern Virginia, but as far as your proposal may affect the Confederate forces under my command, and tend to the restoration of peace, I should be pleased to meet you at 10 A.M. to-mor-row on the old stage-road to Richmond, between the picket-lines of the two armies.   R. E. LEE, *General.*

" ' LIEUTENANT-GENERAL U. S. GRANT.'

" Early on the morning of the 9th I returned him an answer, as follows, and immediately started to join the column north of the Appomattox :

" ' April 9, 1865.

" ' GENERAL,—Your note of yesterday I received.   I have no authority to treat on the subject of peace ; the meeting proposed for 10 A.M. to-day could lead to no good.   I will state, however, general, that I am equally anxious for peace with yourself, and the whole North entertains the same feeling. The terms on which peace can be had are well understood.   By the South laying down their arms they will hasten that most desirable event, save thousands of human lives and hundreds of millions of property not yet destroyed.   Seriously hoping that our difficulties may be settled without the loss of another life, I subscribe myself, etc.,

" ' U. S. GRANT, *Lieutenant-General.*
" ' GENERAL R. E. LEE.'

" On the morning of the 9th General Ord's command of the Fifth Corps reached Appomattox Station just as the enemy was making a desperate effort to break through our cavalry.   The infantry were at once thrown in.   Soon after a white flag was received, requesting a suspension of hostilities pending negotiations for a surrender.   Before reaching General Sheridan's headquar-ters I received the following from General Lee :

" ' April 9, 1865.

" ' GENERAL,—I received your note of this morning on the picket-line, whither I had come to meet you and ascertain definitely what terms were embraced in your proposal of yesterday with reference to the surrender of this army. I now ask an interview in accordance with the offer contained in your letter of yesterday for that purpose.

" ' R. E. LEE, *General.*

" ' LIEUTENANT-GENERAL U. S. GRANT.'

" The interview was held at Appomattox Court-House, the result of which is set forth in the following correspondence:

" ' APPOMATTOX COURT-HOUSE, VA., April 9, 1865.

" ' GENERAL,—In accordance with the substance of my letter to you of the 8th instant, I propose to receive the surrender of the Army of Northern Virginia on the following terms, to wit: Rolls of all the officers and men to be made in duplicate, one copy to be given to an officer to be designated by me, the other to be retained by such officer as you may designate. The officers to give their individual paroles not to take up arms against the government of the United States until properly exchanged, and each company or regimental commander sign a like parole for the men of their commands.

" ' The arms, artillery, and public property to be parked and stacked, and turned over to the officer appointed by me to receive them. This will not embrace the side-arms of the officers, nor their private horses or baggage.

" ' This done, each officer and man will be allowed to return to his home, not to be disturbed by the United States authority so long as they observe their paroles and the laws in force where they reside.

" ' U. S. GRANT, *Lieutenant-General.*

" ' GENERAL R. E. LEE.'

" ' HEADQUARTERS ARMY OF NORTHERN VIRGINIA,

" ' April 9, 1865.

" ' GENERAL,—I received your letter of this date containing the terms of the surrender of the Army of Northern Virginia as proposed by you. As they are substantially the same as those expressed in your letter of the 8th instant, they are accepted. I will proceed to designate the proper officers to carry the stipulations into effect.   R. E. LEE, *General.*

" ' LIEUTENANT-GENERAL U. S. GRANT.'

" The command of Major-General Gibbon, the Fifth Army Corps, under

Griffin, and McKenzie's cavalry were designated to remain at Appomattox Court-House until the paroling of the surrendered army was completed and to take charge of the public property. The remainder of the army returned to the vicinity of Burkesville."

After the surrender was concluded the troops were drawn up, and the commanding generals rode along the lines, congratulating the men on the complete success of their labors and the approaching dawn of a permanent peace. They were lustily cheered by each organization as they passed, and general joy and jubilation reigned supreme, which was also shared in, to a great extent, by very many of the captured rebels.

As soon as the terms of the surrender were arranged and the overthrow of our old and brave antagonist, the Army of Northern Virginia, was an actual fact, our corps marched back to Burkesville, where we enjoyed over two weeks of grateful rest, untroubled by the constant apprehension of orders to march or to attack.

During the active campaign around Petersburg the following-named men of the regiment were killed or died of wounds received in action : at Petersburg there were killed Sergeant Edward Maull, of Company F, and Private John T. Groves, of Company I. At Hatcher's Run, Sergeant Lewis Correll, of Company H, was mortally wounded. At High Bridge, Privates Samuel Cochrane, of Company B, and Peter Shrout, of Company I, were killed, and Privates William Algier, of Company A, and George Wilkins, of Company D, were mortally wounded.

Since December, 1864, the changes among the commissioned officers were as follows; January 1, 1865, First Lieutenant John W. Barney, of Company B, was promoted to captain, and Alfred Nones was appointed first lieutenant of the same company; on the 5th, James Kettlewood was appointed captain of Company H; and on the 9th, Captain David S. Yardley resigned.

February 1st, First Lieutenant William J. Birney, Company D, was promoted to captain; on the 13th, Captain John T. Dent, of Company G, was promoted to major, and Second Lieutenant Henry H. Burton was raised to first lieutenant of Company G; March 15th, Robert E. Russell was made principal musician.

April 20th, Surgeon David W. Maull resigned, feeling that the active work of the regiment was finished, and with his usual modesty, having no desire to share in the popular ovations awaiting the regiment "When Johnny comes Marching Home." All parted from him with sincere regret, even though but few weeks, as it then appeared, would elapse before we should join him at home. On the 29th, Second Lieutenant William Murphey, of Company F, resigned.

MUSTERED OUT.

On the 1st of May the command left Burkesville on its homeward march,—the last long tramp of the war. The column passed through Richmond and Fredericksburg, and went into camp near Munson's Hill on the 15th. The weather was very warm, and this long march was exceedingly severe on the men, many of those who had not been in the service long becoming exhausted and dying, as it were, almost on the very threshold of their homes. This long and fatiguing march at the close of the war was wholly unnecessary. No plea of economy can justify the measure that resulted in the death of so many of the gallant men who had survived the perils of the battle-field. They should have been transported to their homes by water and rail, as they were carried to the front.

At the end of May the Army of the Potomac and Sherman's army marched through Washington in review before the President and all the civic heads of the nation. This was the grandest military pageant the civilized world ever witnessed; for nowhere in the annals of modern history can we find an instance where nearly two hundred thousand victorious veterans marched in review previous to disbanding to the occupations of civil life. The column was so long that two days were required for it to pass a given point, moving in quick time.

The regiment lay in camp in Virginia, nearly opposite Washington, through the month of June, engaged in the preparation of muster-out rolls and returns of public property. In the last two months a number of changes occurred among the commissioned officers: May 15th, Captain George T. Price, of Company C, was discharged; on the 17th, Assistant Surgeon Joseph W. McCullough was promoted to surgeon; on the 20th, Captain William J. Birney, of Company D, resigned; on the 25th, Sergeant William W. Davis, of Company H, was appointed sergeant-major; on the 27th, First Lieutenant Alfred Nones, of Company B, resigned; on the 30th, Sergeant Thomas Russell, of Company B, was promoted to second lieutenant of Company K; and on the 31st, Thomas D. G. Smith was appointed first lieutenant of Company D, and William McCoy second lieutenant; First Lieutenant James M. Bryan, of Company A, was promoted to captain of Company G; Second Lieutenant Joseph E. Booth, of Company B, was advanced to first lieutenant of Company A; Sergeant Michael Dooley, of Company H, was made second lieutenant; and Moses Magee was appointed hospital steward.

On June 9th, Second Lieutenant Russell, of Company K, was transferred to Company H; on the 3d, Second Lieutenant Michael Dooley, of Company H, was transferred to Company K; on the 9th, Sergeant William Marsh, of Company C, was made second lieutenant of Company F; William H. Vining was appointed second lieutenant of Company I, and Dr. Benjamin B. Groves was appointed assistant surgeon; and on the 16th, First Lieutenant Evan P. Grubb, of Company K, was promoted to captain of Company D, and Second Lieutenant William N. Meacham, of Company G, was promoted to first lieutenant of Company K.

All the preparations having been completed, on the 12th of July, 1865, the regiment was mustered out of service at its camp near Munson's Hill, and, under orders from the War Department, took the cars for Wilmington on the 14th of July, where, after being honored by an enthusiastic reception, it was disbanded.

By order of the War Department the following were announced as the battles in which the First Delaware Regiment was engaged: Fair Oaks, Gaines' Mill, Peach Orchard, Savage Station, White Oak Swamp, Malvern Hill,

Antietam, Fredericksburg, Chancellorsville, Gettysburg, Bristoe Station, Mine Run, Wilderness, Spottsylvania, North Anna, Tolopotomoy, Cold Harbor, Petersburg, Deep Bottom, Ream's Station, and Boydton Road.

To this list should be added Auburn, Locust Grove, Po River, Morton's Ford, Strawberry Plains, Hatcher's Run, High Bridge, and Lee's Surrender. The first six battles mentioned in official orders are accredited to the First Delaware by reason of the consolidation with it, July 1, 1864, of a portion of the Second Delaware Regiment, which bore an honorable share in those engagements.

Sergeant John B. Mayberry, of Company F, received a medal of honor from the War Department for gallant and meritorious service.

To those who feel an interest in the first organization that went from Delaware to support and defend the Government, and which furnished so many valuable officers to other regiments from the State, all of which won for themselves a high reputation for patriotism and bravery, the following tables showing the number of commissioned officers borne on the muster-in rolls who were killed, died of disease, resigned, were discharged or transferred, and promoted, and the number that remained to the close of the war; and the number of enlisted men of each company whose names were on the muster-in rolls who were commissioned, killed, died, were reported missing, deserted, or were transferred or discharged; and of those who served until mustered out, will be of great value in disclosing the fate of a thousand men who entered upon a career of such unusual hardship and peril.

COMMISSIONED OFFICERS.

Promoted.	Resigned.	Discharged.	Transferred.	Killed.	Died.	Mustered out.	Total.
2	19	2	3	5	3	4	38

ENLISTED MEN.

COMPANY.	Commissioned.	Discharged.	Transferred.	Killed.	Died.	Deserted.	Missing.	Mustered out.	Total.
A......................	2	49	7	18	3	6	...	10	95
B......................	3	19	7	13	4	10	...	6	62
C......................	4	20	7	9	8	22	...	15	85
D......................	3	37	7	18	9	7	...	12	93
E......................	2	46	8	15	6	5	7	13	102
F......................	9	28	6	10	8	5	2	21	89
G......................	2	40	2	15	6	7	...	6	78
H......................	4	37	8	12	7	6	...	7	81
I......................	3	25	10	9	6	4	1	26	84
K......................	6	31	1	8	2	6	...	15	69
	38	332	63	127	59	78	10	131	838

These tables are compiled from the muster-out rolls, and it will be readily seen that, in most of the companies, all the men who marched from Wilmington with the regiment have not been accounted for, and their fate is not shown. In these statistics none of the men who joined the regiment by transfer, or as recruits, substitutes, or conscripts, have been taken into account, the object being to show only what became of the officers and men of the organization as it was mustered in.

The story of the achievements and sacrifices of the First Regiment Delaware Volunteers in the great war of the Rebellion is now told, briefly and imperfectly, since the limits of a historical sketch are too narrow to permit the glorious deeds these heroic men have carved upon the tablets of our national history to be recited in the glowing word-pictures they so eminently deserve.

Let us hope that coming generations, when they assemble to congratulate themselves on the liberty, happiness, and prosperity they enjoy, will not fail to honor the memories of the daring men who paused not to consider selfish interests, who hesitated over no personal sacrifices, with nothing mercenary to tempt them in the form of large bounty, no State military laws, even, on which to depend for clothing, shelter, and subsistence while organizing; yet, when powerful and thoroughly-organized treason clutched the throat of the nation, and it cried out in its agony, "Save me or I die!" they sprang to the front, seized their weapons, fought the traitors to the death, aided in the delivery of their country, and when the enemy was stretched out exhausted and harmless, they laid down their arms and returned modestly to their former stations of industrious and law-abiding citizens.

INDEX.

Sheridan, Philip H., 137, 142, 143, 145, 146.
Sherman, William T., 150.
Shortledge, Allen, 27, 51, 94.
Shrout, Peter, 148.
Shulty, John, 90.
Sickness in the camp, 36, 43.
Simpson, James, Company B, 72, 90.
Simpson, James, Company F, 52.
Simpson, James D., 64, 94, 116.
Simpson, Samuel, 15.
Simpson, Thomas A., 52.
Sinnox, Thomas, 60.
Sixth Army Corps, The, 115, 117, 128.
Skirmish beyond Hampton, 35.
Skirmishing, 54, 56, 59, 80, 85, 88, 92, 96, 100, 102, 132, 143.
Slavery, 5.
Slaves in Delaware, Number of, 6.
Smith, D. G., 72.
Smith, George F., 15, 18.
Smith, John H., 52.
Smith, Thomas D. G., 150.
Smith, William, Company A, 64, 65, 82, 87, 88, 89.
Smith, William, Company B, 60.
Smith, William F., 26, 37, 53, 60, 69, 70, 71, 95, 104, 132, 134.
Smithers, Enoch J., 15, 26, 37.
Smyrna, Del., 93.
Smyth, Thomas A., 26, 36, 38, 42, 45, 48, 51, 56, 57, 59, 61, 64, 67, 69, 71, 75, 77, 82, 83, 84, 87, 90, 93, 96, 99, 102, 104, 105, 111, 113, 114, 117, 119, 122, 129, 130, 131, 132, 133, 135, 136, 141, 142.
Sneider, George, 60.
Social intercourse with the enemy, 62.
Soldiers' Christian Association, The, 31.
South Side Railroad, The, 138, 142.
Southall House, The, 128, 129.
Sparks, John L., 27, 53, 64, 70, 99.
Spicer, Philip R., 52.
"Spot," the colonel's horse, 51.
Spottsylvania Court-House, The battles at, 105.
    Mentioned, 109, 110, 112, 115, 122, 152.
Springfield, Va., 92.
Sprogle, Mr., 19.
Staff-officers appointed, 17, 26.
Stafford Court-House, Va., 78.
"State of Maine," The transport, 46.
Steel, Charles J., 72, 108.
Stein, John, 90.
Stemmer's Run, 19.
Stevensburg, Va., 102.
Stewart, G. H., 110
Stony Mountain, Va., 103, 104.
Strawberry Plains, Va., 119, 152.
Sudley Springs, Va., 79.

Suffolk, Va., 43, 44, 45.
Sumner, Edwin V., 46.
Supporting batteries, 69.
Surrender of General Lee, The, 144.
Susquehanna River, The, 19.
Sussex County, Del., 6.
Sweeney, Hugh, 26, 43.
Sweeney, Thomas M., 52.
Swiggett, William Y., 15, 27, 51, 63, 103.
Sylvester, Levi, 44.

Taneytown, Md., 80, 85, 88, 90.
Tanner, Charles B., 37, 40, 48, 49, 51, 55, 70, 94, 141.
Tanner, John B., 27, 34, 65.
Tanner's Creek, 41.
Tatem, Allen, 33, 49, 63, 64, 121.
Tenth Army Corps, The, 119, 130.
Theatre erected, A, 32.
Third Army Corps, The, 66, 70.
Thomas, Robert, 116.
Thompson, Jacob H., 72.
Thompson, John, 139.
Thompson, Richard S., 84, 85.
Thornton, Thomas, 108.
Tilghmanton, Md., 91.
Todd's Tavern, Va., 66, 105, 109.
Tolopotomoy, The battle of, 113.
    Mentioned, 113, 116, 126, 152.
Tomes, Mr., 19.
Torbert, William F. A., 74.
Truce declared, A, 114.
Turkey Creek, 96, 98.
Turner's Gap, Md., 46.
Twelfth Army Corps, The, 81.
Twenty-fourth Army Corps, The, 133.
Two Taverns, Md., 90.
Tyler, General, 75.

Union Bridge, Md., 79.
Uniontown, Md., 79, 85.
United States Ford, Va., 65, 69, 70, 74, 76.
Upperville, Va., 92.
Urbana, Md., 46, 79.

Van Trump, Isaac, 27, 42.
Vandever, Alfred, 15.
Vanloan, John R., 27, 37.
Vaughan, William D., 77.
Veteran furlough, The, 103.
Veteran Reserve Corps, The, 103, 104.
Viele, Egbert L., 43.
Vincent, Peter W., 72.
Vining, William H., 151.

Wainright, Mr., 20.
Wales, Leonard E., 15.
Walker, John J., 52.
Wallace, Gustave A., 116.

THE END.

GETTYSBURG TITLES

These Honored Dead: The Union Casualties at Gettysburg, RE-VISED EDITION, by John W. Busey. Full listing of all 5101 killed and mortally wounded, listed by state and regiment, plus complete alphabetical index. A definitive study that gives age, enlistment data, nature of wound, and burial data. New edition contains 100 extra pages and over 20 new photographs of casualties. 508 pages, over 40 illustrations. Hard bound. Published 1996. $30.00.

The Last Full Measure: Burials in the Soldiers' National Cemetery at Gettysburg, by John Busey. The only published index to the cemetery; contains corrected name listings. 277 pages, 7 illustrations, map. Hard bound. Published 1988. $20.00.

Regimental Strengths and Losses at Gettysburg, THIRD EDITION, by John Busey and Dr. David Martin. Revised and Corrected edition of this highly respected study. Contains order of battle and strength infirmation not available elsewhere. Detailed comparative strength and loss tables. 360 pages, indices. Hard bound. Published 1994. $20.00.

Final Report of the New Jersey Gettysburg Battlefield Monument Commission. Reprint of scarce 1891 government report. Gives excellent background on the erection of the monuments and their dedication ceremonies. 194 pages, numerous illustrations, index; 1 new map added. Published 1997. $20.00.

New Jersey Troops in the Gettysburg Campaign, by Samuel Toombs. Reprint of 1888 edition, with new introduction and index by Dr. David Martin. 440 pages. Hard bound. Published 1988. $30.00.

Address Delivered at the Rededication of the Monument to the First New Jersey Brigade at Gettysburg, October 9, 1982, by Dr. David Martin. 12 page booklet. Published 1992. $3.50.

Holding the Left at Gettysburg: The 20th N.Y.S.M. on July 1, 1863, by Seward Osborne. A well received original booklet. 36 pages, 2 maps, 6 photographs. Published 1990. $6.00.

OTHER BOOKS BY LONGSTREET HOUSE

History of the First Regiment Delaware Volunteers, by Alexander Seville. Enhanced reprint of 1884 edition. 163 pages, index. Hard bound. Published 1998. $20.00.

My Sons were Faithful and They Fought: The Irish Brigade at Antietam, An Anthology, edited by Joseph Bilby and Steve O'Neill. Collection of essays by several noted authors. Royalties will go to support the new Irish brigade monument dedicated in September 1997 at Antietam. 140 pages, 30 illustrations, 5 maps. Softbound, oversize, attractive color covers. Published July 1997. $18.00.

The Civil War Diaries of Col. Theodore B. Gates, Twentieth New York State Militia, edited by Seward Osborne. This regiment from Ulster County served in the First Corps at Antietam and Gettysburg and then in the Army of the Potomac's Provost Guard. 197 pages, 35 illustrations, 11 maps, index. Hard bound. Published 1992. $25.00.

The Plymouth Pilgrims: A History of the Eighty-Fifth New York Infantry in the Civil War, by Wayne Mahood. Revised edition of our 1989 book, which quickly sold out. The regiment fought in North Carolina and was captured almost intact at Plymouth and then sent to Andersonville Prison. 367 pages, expanded roster, 15 maps, over 100 illustrations. Hard bound. Published 1992. $30.00.

Charlie Mosher's Civil War: From Fair Oaks to Anderson vale with the Plymouth Pilgrims (85th N.Y. Inf.), edited by Wayne Mahood. Gives new insights into the war on the North Carolina coast, plus a very moving account of prison life at Andersonville and Florence. 350 pages, 30 illustrations, indices. Hard bound. Published June 1994. $30.00.

Written in Blood: A History of the 126th New York Infantry in the Civil War, by Wayne Mahood. An all-new annotated history, with roster. Great content on Gettysburg and 1864 Virginia Campaigns. 548 pages, 20 maps, 63 illustrations including portraits of 23 unit members. Published 1997. $40.00.

The Saga of the Mountain Legion (156th N.Y. Vols.) of "The Modest Hero Who Saved Our Flag", by Seward Osborne. The first study of this unit. from Ulster County. 40 page booklet, 10 illustrations. Published 1994. $6.00.

Enlisted for the War: The Struggles of the Gallant 24th Regiment South Carolina Volunteers, 1861-1865, by Eugene Jones. An all-new annotated history with full descriptive roster. 528 pages, 17 maps, 40 illustrations including portraits of 20 unit members. Published 1997. $40.00.

Order from Longstreet House, PO Box 730, Hightstown, NJ 08520
Postage $3.00 per order. N. J. residents kindly include tax.